how2become

*How to Pass The Police*
*Inspector Application*
*Process: Direct Entry*

**www.How2Become.com**

As part of this product you have also received FREE access to online tests that will help you to pass your Police Inspector tests.

To gain access, simply go to:

**www.PsychometricTestsOnline.co.uk**

Get more products for passing any test at:

**www.How2Become.com**

Orders: Please contact How2Become Ltd, Suite 14, 50 Churchill Square Business Centre, Kings Hill, Kent ME19 4YU.

You can order through Amazon.co.uk under ISBN: 9781911259862, via the website www.How2Become.com or through Gardners.com.

ISBN: 9781911259862

First published in 2017 by How2Become Ltd.

Typeset by Gemma Butler for How2Become Ltd.

## Disclaimer

Every effort has been made to ensure that the information contained within this guide is accurate at the time of publication. How2Become Ltd is not responsible for anyone failing any part of any selection process as a result of the information contained within this guide. How2Become Ltd and their authors cannot accept any responsibility for any errors or omissions within this guide, however caused. No responsibility for loss or damage occasioned by any person acting, or refraining from action, as a result of the material in this publication can be accepted by How2Become Ltd.

The information within this guide does not represent the views of any third-party service or organisation.

# Contents

# INTRODUCTION

Hello, and welcome to *How to Pass The Police Inspector Application Process: Direct Entry*. As you might have guessed, in this book we'll be teaching you all about how to ace the direct entry police inspector application process. From the application form, all the way through to the assessment centre itself, we'll provide you with our expert insight on what you can expect, and the best way to prepare for it. Along with this, we've also provided you with numerous practice tests, to help you improve your ability. By the end of this guide, you will be in a fantastic position to tackle the police inspector application process.

Let's start by looking at the role itself.

**What is a Police Inspector?**

A police inspector plays an extremely important role in the day-to-day running of the police service. Inspectors serve as middle managers, who are tasked with supervising established members of the police force, such as constables and sergeants. As an inspector, you will be responsible for the planning of essential police work, and must be able to conduct tasks such as:

- Using police resources to full effect;

- Managing major incidents and investigations;

- Monitoring the performance of your staff;

- Conducting regular reviews of police practice, to ensure that the service is working to its maximum potential, and to identify possible improvements.

Police inspectors don't just work for the police service. The British Transport Police and the Ministry of Defence both make full use of police inspectors, in their day-to-day activities.

In recent times, the best way to become a police inspector was through working in the force itself, and rising through the ranks. While this is still a very viable method, the police have now introduced a new system, to help capable individuals reach the rank of inspector. This system is known as **Direct Entry.**

## Direct Entry

The Direct Entry Inspector programme is a 24-month, comprehensive training course, which will teach you everything that you need to know about working as an inspector. By the end of the course, you will be qualified to work as an operational inspector. You don't need to have worked within the police service to take this course, although it is essential that you can demonstrate skills and qualities such as:

- Leadership;

- Management;

- Ambition;

- Resilience;

- Flexibility.

If this sounds easy enough, think again. As we've mentioned, police inspectors play a fundamental role in the service, and therefore you can't just stroll onto the course. In order to get a place on the Direct Entry programme, you'll need to pass an extremely tough application process. You'll face challenges such as a competency-based application form, interviews, and even a gruelling assessment centre. The police service want to ensure that only the very best candidates are taking part in the programme, and for this reason, they've made the application process as tough as possible!

The stages that you will face during the application process, are as follows:

- **Online recruitment questionnaire.** This test is not marked, but is simply provided to give you a better idea of what to expect. In the next chapter, we'll provide you with some useful tips on how to analyse your own score in this assessment, and the best way to approach the questions;

- **Online application form.** The next stage is an online application form. This is an extremely in-depth form, where you will be asked to answer a number of important questions. Along with providing personal details about your background, you will need to answer **competency-based questions**. Later in this guide, we'll give you a full breakdown of how to respond to these;

- **Telephone interview.** The penultimate stage of the process is a telephone interview. You'll speak to a member of the police service on the phone, for a period of roughly 30-45 minutes. The interviewer will ask you questions based on the answers in your application form, about your background, and quiz you about your knowledge of the role;

- **Assessment centre.** Finally, if you pass all of the previous stages, you will be invited to attend an assessment centre. Unlike other assessment centres that you might have experienced or have knowledge of, this assessment centre will take place over a couple of days. You'll take a wide range of tests, and will conclude the assessment centre with a face-to-face interview.

## Eligibility and Other Information

Before we move onto the core competencies and the first stages of the application process, there are some key facts that you need to know about applying for the course. As you might have gathered from what we have already told you, the Direct Entry programme is only open to the very best candidates, which is why applicants need to go through such an extensive application process. In addition to this, there are further restrictions on who can apply for the role, otherwise known as the eligibility criteria. Below we've provided a summary of what requirements you'll need to meet, and some other important facts that you'll need to know about the course.

## Age Limit

The upper age limit for applicants to this programme is 57. You must be 18 or older to apply. Candidates for the Direct Entry programme can apply as many times as they want. However, should you fail the assessment centre twice, you will need to wait a total of 5 years before applying again.

## Nationality/Residency

Candidates from outside the EEA must have leave to remain in the UK for an indefinite period, without restrictions. The police require a three-year history when vetting, meaning that you will need to have been a resident of the UK for three years prior to application.

## Tattoos

The police have a very strict policy on tattoos and piercings. Tattoos and piercings are not deemed acceptable by the police, if they:

- Are seen as undermining the dignity of the employee;
- Risk causing offence to members of the public, or police staff;
- Are particularly garish/prominent;
- Could be seen as discriminatory to any group of people.

## Finances

When applying to join the police, your financial history will be considered. You will not be accepted if you have an existing County Court judgement against your name, or if you have remaining debts that are a result of bankruptcy. Likewise, you will be rejected if you are the subject of an Individual Voluntary Agreement.

Candidates who have been previously registered as bankrupt, will only be considered if they have been discharged from their debt for a period of three years prior to application.

## Eyesight

In order to successfully apply, you will need to meet the eyesight requirements. The requirements are as follows:

- You must be at a level of 6/12 or better in either eye, or 6/6 with both eyes together, when testing long distance vision;
- You must be at a level of 6/9 with both eyes together, when testing near vision;
- The police do not accept the use of colour correcting lenses. Nor do they accept radial keratotomy, arcuate keratotomy or corneal grafts.

## Probation

Once you have been accepted onto the course, you will be on a period of probation for the duration of the programme. This means that you will need to prove to the assessors that you have what it takes to succeed in the role, or risk being removed from the programme. All candidates who successfully complete the programme are guaranteed an offer of employment.

## Chosen Constabulary

The application process allows candidates to apply for more than one force. On the application form, you will be asked to list your preferred ranking of the forces that are taking part in the programme/which of these you would like to work for. If you do receive a place on the programme, then this list will be used to determine which force you might work for.

## Past Convictions

As you would expect, the police are very strict on the criminal history of their candidates. Below we've included all of the information on how past criminal convictions could impact your application.

When considering criminal convictions, each case will be judged based on its own merits, and therefore it is up to the police to decide on whether the exact past conviction will prohibit you from joining. That being said, applications will not be accepted if a candidate (of any age) has previously been convicted or cautioned for:

- Murder;
- Treason;
- Manslaughter;
- Rape;
- Incest;
- Offences that fall under the sexual offences act of 2003;
- Sexual activity with a child;
- Hostage-taking or torture;
- Involvement in espionage or terrorism;
- Any driving offences which have resulted in a death;
- Firearms offences;
- Domestic violence offences.

Similarly, you are highly unlikely to be accepted if you have been convicted or cautioned on charges of:

- Violence;
- GBH;
- ABH;
- Unlawful possession of firearms;
- Gross indecency;
- Abuse or neglect of children;
- Public order offences;
- Burglary;
- Fraud;
- Any offence which involved acting in a dishonest or corrupt manner, invoking loss to others involved;
- Possession with, or involvement in, class A drugs or class B drugs;
- Reckless or dangerous driving within the 10 years preceding application, including drink driving or driving under the influence of drugs;
- Convictions that are a result of driving without insurance, in the past 5 years. Likewise, failing to stop after an accident.

Your age at the time of offence, and other circumstances, will be taken into consideration for the following cases:

- Being drunk and disorderly;
- Minor drugs offences or substance abuse;
- Common assault;
- If you have outstanding charges or court summon requests;
- If you have been convicted of an offence by a military tribunal;
- If relatives or associates of the applicant are found to have engaged in activity which could lead to embarrassment for the police, or risk

discrediting the police as an organisation.

## Substance Misuse

As per standard police regulations, you will need to take a substance misuse test during the application process. Failure to take part in this, or failure of the misuse test, will result in you being removed from the process.

## Shift Work

You will need to be prepared to work shifts. Shift work is an essential part of policing, and there are times when you will need to work at nights and at weekends. You will be required to work approximately 40 hours per week.

## Education/Past Employment

Having a degree may benefit you in the application process, although it is not essential. There are no educational qualifications required in order to apply, and candidates will be judged based on how well they meet the police criteria, and not on their academic background. Existing police employees are welcome to apply, and will face the same tests as everyone else. That being said, existing employees are eligible to participate in a Fast Track programme, which accelerates the process.

## Salary

Candidates who are accepted on the programme will receive a salary of approximately £48,000 a year, from the very start of the course. This could, however, vary between forces.

## The Programme

The programme lasts for a period of 24 months. You'll spend the majority of your time working in operational rotation, and the rest taking part in lessons. The programme is free, and you won't have to pay anything towards it. The course will be assessed via a variety of methods, including examinations, work-based supervision and participation in operational and community projects.

So, now that we've looked at the basic requirements, and what the role of an inspector is, let's move onto the police inspector core competencies.

# POLICE INSPECTOR CORE COMPETENCIES

Just as with the normal police application process, the Direct Entry Inspector programme makes full use of a set of core competencies. If you aren't familiar with core competencies, check out the below explanation:

Core competencies are a set of behavioural characteristics. The majority of employers use core competencies as a guideline for how they expect their employees to work. This can differ between sectors. For example, if you were working in an art shop, one of your core competencies might be the ability to sell products to customers. Obviously, this is not going to be the case when working for the police, who will use different core competencies.

Core competencies are not just important for when you are working on the job, but are also important during the application process. At every single stage, the assessors will be judging you based on how well you meet the core competencies. Every answer will be carefully analysed, to judge whether you have demonstrated a knowledge and awareness of the competencies. The core competencies ensure that everyone working within the police force has clear standards to follow, and understands what is expected of them.

Now, let's look at the core competencies required for a police inspector, and a number of other key behaviours too.

## Emotional Awareness

Emotional awareness is all about having the ability to understand others, and yourself. As an inspector, you will need to be someone who can engage with and listen to others, making a concentrated effort to understand their needs and perspectives.

It's also important that inspectors can manage their emotions in difficult situations, and understand why you are making certain decisions. By acting in an emotionally sensitive way, you can ensure that you are meeting the cultural demands of different groups of people, and dealing with them in the right manner. Having empathy is integral to police work.

Emotional awareness is important, as it has a big impact on the way that the public perceive the police. Not only will emotional awareness help you when dealing directly with the public, but it will also have an impact on your relationship with your colleagues. The better you can work as part of the team, the better service you can provide for the general public.

**A person with good emotional awareness will:**

- Treat every person whom they meet with tolerance and respect;

- Remain calm in tense situations, especially when provoked;

- Understand which situations are likely to trigger an irrational or emotional response, from themselves and others;

- Make sustained efforts to understand the thoughts and feelings of others;

- Be able to empathise;

- Promote the values of respect and diversity;

- Take responsibility for the emotional wellbeing of others.

## Takes Ownership

Taking ownership and responsibility is a very important quality for police inspectors to have. It's essential that you can hold yourself accountable for mistakes that are made, without letting this hold you back from taking necessary risks. As an inspector, you are a decision maker. Crime and crime solving is an unpredictable field, where things could change in an instant. Thus, not all of your decisions will work out, but you must be prepared to back the decisions that you have made, with clear rationale. When mistakes are made, it's important to learn from the experience, accept feedback and reflect, to improve future practice.

Taking ownership also means having the confidence to make tough decisions, which won't necessarily be within your comfort zone. It's about taking responsibility, and generating confidence in your decision-making abilities, from both others and yourself.

**A person who takes ownership will:**

- Identify and respond proactively to problems;

- Ensure that their decisions are based on the fundamental principle of public service;

- Take feedback into account, to improve the quality of their work;

- Take responsibility for their actions;

- Encourage others to also take responsibility for their own decisions and behaviour;

- Hold themselves accountable for the behaviour of their team;

- Behave in a way befitting a role model within the police force;

- Help others to improve their performance, via constructive feedback;

- Take responsibility for initiating improvements across the entire police force.

## Works Collaboratively

Working collaboratively is extremely important within the police. In order to ensure the safety of the public, it's vital that the police can work as an efficient and organised unit. As such, police inspectors and employees must be able to look past personal disagreements and feelings, and work together to produce the best possible outcome for the public.

As an inspector, it's important that you can work with your colleagues, to build long-lasting and amicable relationships. This extends to building relationships with external operators and other public sector organisations, all of whom could be extremely useful. By working with these organisations, inspectors can ensure that they are sharing and receiving knowledge and essential insights, thereby increasing the capacity of all parties to serve the general public.

It's a known fact that the demands on the police service are increasing every single year, and becoming more diverse in nature. This means that the police need to think ambitiously about how they solve problems, and identify solutions which don't just help a minority, but work for all concerned parties. By ensuring that everyone is provided with the same level of safeguarding and protection, the police can guarantee the trust and respect of the public.

**A person who works collaboratively can:**

- Work in a cooperative manner, to get tasks completed with the help of colleagues;

- Project an approachable persona, thereby encouraging the confidence of colleagues;

- Listen to the views and opinions of others, and make a concerted attempt to understand their perspective;

- Treat others in a respectful and fair manner, taking their viewpoints into consideration;

- Work without making assumptions about different people, based on previous experience. Treats every person as a unique circumstance/case;

- Develop a sustained political understanding, and the impact that various laws and decisions have on both the public, and alternative sectors to the police;

- Contribute to an environment where teamworking and collaboration are consistently seen as the best solutions to problems.

## Deliver, Support and Inspire

As an inspector, it's essential that you understand the core vision and values of the police force, and are able to use these during your day-to-day operations. Let's have a look at all three terms, and what they mean:

**Deliver** – Delivery means providing what is promised to the public. In this case: safeguarding and protection. The better you can meet all of the competencies, the better service you can provide.

**Support** – Supporting applies to both the public, and your colleagues. As an inspector, you won't just need to provide guidance and assurance to the general public, but also to your own staff.

**Inspire** – Police employees are role models, and this is especially true for higher ranking police employees – such as inspectors. Not only are police expected to set an example for the public, by behaving in a law-abiding manner, but for their own colleagues too.

As an inspector, you will be expected to motivate your staff to perform to the highest possible standards.

**A person who can deliver, support and inspire, will:**

- Have a good understanding of how their role fits into the wider spectrum of police work;

- Take a conscientious approach to their work, making a concerted endeavour to overcome obstacles which could prevent delivery of the best possible service;

- Stay up to date with relevant changes and procedural guidelines;

- Act as a role model for police staff, and for the public;

- Motivate and inspire other police employees to achieve exemplary standards of work and behaviour;

- Utilise strategic and logical thinking, to ensure that the police force can provide the best possible service to the wider public.

## Critical Analysis

Critical analysis is extremely important for police inspectors. As an inspector, you will be required to analyse a wide number of fields, including: data, evidence, reports and statements, in your quest to make the UK a safer place to live. In doing so, you will need to draw from the experience that you have picked up in the police, and any evidence available, to try and glean a concise overview of the facts. As always, an evidence based approach is the best one to take.

Police inspectors will use critical analysis on a daily basis, as a way of dealing with the issues that land on their desk. Many of these issues will be far too complex to be resolved without the use of in-depth critical analysis. As you can see, working as an inspector will require you to be a logical, reliable and responsible decision maker.

**A person who can critically analyse, will:**

- Identify when and where issues need to be critically analysed;

- Assess information in an efficient and logical manner;

- Solve problems using logic and reasoning;

- Make decisions which are in line with the police values and ethics;

- Understand how to balance action with reasoning;

- Be willing to explore alternative and creative problem solving methods;

- Recognise that certain decisions could constitute or cause significant change within the workplace, and that you may need to justify these decisions to higher ranking employees than yourself.

## Innovative and Open-Minded

In order to work as an inspector, it's imperative that you can take an innovative and open-minded approach. Inspectors should always be looking to improve, and this means that you must constantly be on the lookout for new methods and improvements on your current working practice. When working for the police, it's important that you can take a flexible and adaptable approach. The police force are constantly changing their methods, in order to keep up with crime, meaning that an open-mind will go a long way to helping you in this position.

**A person who is innovative and open-minded will:**

- Welcome new ideas, ways of working and creative solutions;

- Share suggestions and feedback with colleagues;

- Take a flexible approach to problems;

- Learn from their experiences, and enter each situation without judgement or preconception;

- Take the lead in implementing new and creative working practices, which could have a radical and positive impact on the way the police force functions;

- Encourage others to think flexibly, and discuss their ideas;

- Do their utmost to ensure that the police is as up-to-date as possible, so that they can provide the best possible service to the public.

Along with these competencies, inspectors are also expected to follow certain values:

## Values

### Integrity

It's extremely important for police employees to act with integrity at all times, and this of course extends to inspectors. As an inspector, you will be high ranking within the police force, and therefore will be expected to set a good example for other employees. You are a role model, and therefore you must embody the values and expectations of the police force, down to a tee. Remember that the police have a duty of care to the public, and part of maintaining this involves building up a good level of trust with the public, and a good reputation for the police in general. With this in mind, integrity is extremely important. If you don't act with integrity, then you can't expect the public to respect or trust you. Integrity means taking an honest, unbiased and professional approach to every single situation that you encounter, supporting and delivering upon the expectations that the public have of the police, and working in a collaborative manner with both the public and other members of the police force. Along with this, you need to remember that although being a police inspector puts you in a position of authority – it's important to ensure that you are respectful and mindful of the influence of your position. Don't take advantage of your position, and treat other members of staff with respect and fairness, whilst remaining open to criticism and advice from your fellow police employees.

### Public Service

Public service is extremely important for the police, as it essentially forms the basis for everything that they do. As a member of the police force, it is your job to protect the public. Whether you are patrolling the streets or working back at police HQ, you need to be someone who believes 100% in doing what is right for the public. This means developing on skills such as customer service, communication and problem solving, in order to ensure that you can offer the best possible level of service to the public. You need to understand the expectations and needs of different communities, and take steps to address these, on an organisational basis. Your responsibility won't just be dealing with the public, but ensuring that other employees adhere to public expectations. You'll need to build confidence in the police, by talking with people in local communities to explore their viewpoints, and breaking down barriers between them and the police. You must be able to understand the impact and benefits of policing for different communities, and identify the best way to deliver services to them. Remember that there will always be barriers to overcome when solving crime, and it is your job as an inspector to find the best solutions to these.

## Transparency

Transparency roughly translates as honesty. As a police inspector, you have a duty to behave in a way that reflects the ethical standards of the police service, and this means acting with honesty and integrity at all times. You must be able to behave in an ethical and honest manner, and challenge any unprofessional conduct or discriminatory behaviour. Along with this, you must be able to remain calm and professional whilst under pressure, and be prepared to step forward and take control when required. As a police inspector, you are a leader within the force, and this means that those below you and above you must be able to look to you for guidance and reassurance. By maintaining an honest, fair and professional approach, you can ensure that your colleagues, and the public, will trust in you. Transparency links closely with communication. You need to be open and comprehensive when communicating with other individuals, along with being able to maintain confidentiality when necessary.

## Impartiality

Impartiality is really important for a police inspector, or anyone working within the force for that matter. As an employee of the police, you have a duty to treat every single person that you meet in an unbiased and fair manner. You must act without discrimination and prejudice, and only judge people based on the situation, and not on any preconceived values that you might have. Remember that police employees are there to serve all members of the public, regardless of their gender, race or background. You must not allow your personal views to jeopardise police operations. By treating every single person that you meet in a polite and respectful way, you can ensure that the public trust the police, thereby improving the force's reputation; and making crime solving easier as a whole. Every decision that you make as a police inspector must be based on clear rationale and reasoning, with evidence to back it up.

As we have explained, these competencies and behaviours will be essential during the application process. At every stage, you will need to try your utmost to demonstrate them as much as possible. The better you can demonstrate the competencies, the better you will score, and the higher your chances of getting the job.

Now that we've looked at the core competencies, let's move onto the pre-application questionnaire.

### The Pre-Application Questionnaire

The first stage of the application process, is to complete the pre-application questionnaire. This is a short questionnaire, which won't be marked. The aim of the questionnaire is to provide you with an insight into working as a police inspector. You'll be given a series of questions, which will quiz you based on general police-related subjects. You should answer these questions as honestly as possible. At the end of the test, you'll be given a score, indicating whether your answers match the profile required for an inspector. If you score low on this test, you'll be given a recommendation that you reconsider applying for the programme. That being said, even if you score low, you are still welcome to apply – the answers for this test won't be analysed by the assessors, or taken into account when it comes to your overall progression. The test is simply there to help you decide whether this is the right programme for you.

A typical question in this test might look something like this:

---

**Financial Awareness**

*One of the most important elements of working as a leader within the police service is being able to handle the current financial restrictions that are in place. Budget reductions are something that all staff members will need to deal with and consider when planning operations.*

*Having read the above, are you someone who is confident in your financial management skills, who is able to apply these skills to leadership-based tasks?*

**Never -  Rarely – Occasionally – Often – Always**

---

As you can see, you've been given a scale upon which to answer. Obviously, the best answer in this scenario is to say 'always'…but that doesn't mean you should automatically select this. You need to think long and hard about your responses, and whether they accurately reflect your actual capabilities. As mentioned, the test is there to indicate whether you would be a good fit for the programme. It's there to help you. The police don't want you to waste your time applying for the role, if you can't match the capabilities.

Let's look at another sample question, that you might see in the test:

---

**Integrity and Ethics**

*One of the core expectations of the police, is that you can act with integrity at all times. This is especially true for inspectors, who need to set an example for other police staff, and must be able to deal with issues such as discipline and misconduct, in a fair and ethical manner.*

*Having read the above, are you someone who is able to behave with integrity, in all circumstances?*

**Never - Rarely – Occasionally – Often – Always**

---

As you can see, the above question is directly testing you on one of the values of a police inspector – integrity. Once again, the best answer is 'always', but you shouldn't answer with this unless you are certain of it. Remember that this test isn't being scored by the assessors, it's only there to help you decide, and therefore honesty is the best approach. It's important to ensure that you are signing up for the right programme. Even though you aren't being scored by the assessors, you should still take the final mark of this questionnaire seriously, and use it as an indication of whether this is the right thing for you.

Now that we've covered the pre-application questionnaire, let's move onto the application form itself.

**Police Inspector Application Form**

Following the pre-application questionnaire, you'll be invited to fill in the online inspector application form. As you might have guessed, this will be an application form that requires you to enter extensive personal details, as well as answering a series of competency-based questions.

The application form is an extremely important stage, so you need to take it seriously. This is your first point of contact/chance to create a first impression, so make it count! It's a good idea to study the eligibility criteria before you fill in this form. That way, you'll know if your personal details and background match against the core requirements for the role. In this chapter, we'll give you a run through of exactly what you'll encounter in the application form, and how to answer the competency-based questions!

---

**<u>Application Form</u>**

**Personal Details**

Title -

First name -

Surname -

Middle name -

DOB -

Town and country of birth -

Nationality -

Sex -

Ethnic Origin -

National Insurance Number -

Address Line 1 -

Address Line 2 -

(Is this your current address? Yes/No)

Town/City -

County -

Postcode -

Country -

Home telephone number -

Mobile telephone number -

Mobile country code -

Email address -

*Please note that this email will be used for all application correspondence, therefore it is essential that you provide us with an email which you can regularly access.

Driving licence number and category -

---

**Station of Preference**

The following forces are all participating in the Direct Entry Inspector Programme. In order of preference, please rank these forces, with number 1 being your preferred choice. If there are any forces from which you would like to categorically exclude yourself from working, please select N/A.

*Please note that in order to be considered for Gwent, you must be able to speak Welsh to a Level 2 standard. In order to join the Metropolitan Police, you must be able to meet the London residency criteria.

- Cleveland
- Derbyshire
- Dorset
- Gloucestershire
- Greater Manchester
- Gwent
- Hampshire
- Humberside and South Yorkshire
- Lancashire
- Metropolitan Police
- North Wales
- Northamptonshire
- Northumbria
- Suffolk
- Thames Valley
- Warwickshire and West Mercia
- West Midlands
- West Yorkshire

## Further Eligibility Questions

Can you confirm that you meet the nationality requirements that are expected of an applicant to this course?

**Yes/No**

Have you resided in the United Kingdom for a continuous period, for 3 years prior to your application?

**Yes/No**

Have you ever been convicted for an offence, or received a formal caution by the police? This includes any bind-overs which have been imposed by a court of law, traffic convictions, motoring or disorder penalties, anti-social behaviour orders, appearances before a court martial and any juvenile cautions.

**Yes/No**

Are you the subject of any impending prosecutions?

**Yes/No**

Have you ever been involved in a criminal investigation, or been associated with criminal individuals?

**Yes/No**

Do you have any tattoos, which could be deemed offensive or contradictory to the police regulations on tattoos/body ink?

**Yes/No**

Are you currently or have you ever been a member of the British National Party, Combat 18 or the National Front?

**Yes/No**

Do you currently play an active role in politics?

**Yes/No**

Do you, your partner or any relatives currently participate in any business activities, which could prevent or cause problems with your application?

**Yes/No**

Have you been declared bankrupt during the three years prior to this application?

**Yes/No**

Are you the subject of an ongoing Individual Voluntary Arrangement, or are there currently any existing Country Court judgements against your name?

**Yes/No**

## Competency-Based Questions

Along with the above eligibility questions, you may also be asked to provide details of previous employment, and your education. Following this, you'll need to answer the competency-based questions.

Competency-based questions are a series of questions that are designed to test how well you understand and have researched the core requirements of the police. As we've mentioned, the competencies are extremely important, and therefore it's no surprise that you are being tested on them even at this early stage. Although it's obviously essential that you can meet the core eligibility requirements, this is also your first chance to create a great impression with the assessors, and show them that you are the right person for the role.

Don't be surprised if you are expected to answer several questions on these topics. For example, you might be asked a question focusing around leadership. Leadership isn't a core competency of the role, but it does fall under almost every single one of the competencies, and is something that will expected of you when working as a police inspector. Likewise, you could be asked questions focusing around qualities such as organisation, teamwork, resilience or financial awareness. Make sure that before you complete the application form, you have read through the requirements of an inspector **thoroughly**, so that you won't be blindsided by anything on there.

Now, let's look at some sample competency-based questions.

**Q1. In 200 words or less, describe how impartiality is integral to the role of a police inspector.**

## How to Answer

As you might have noticed, this question requires you to answer in 200 words or less. This is standard practice for many police application forms, including the inspector form. Although the inspector form won't always ask you to do this (depending on the year that you are applying) there is a good chance that you will need to provide short and succinct answers to these questions, so be prepared! When you answer this question, remember not to just 'answer the question'. Along with explaining why impartiality is important for police inspectors, you also need to give a (brief) explanation of how you meet or can demonstrate this value, and why it's important to you. The key to a good response is in linking your own behaviour with the core expectations of the force. Let's look at a good sample response to this question:

## Sample Response

*Having conducted thorough research into the role of a police inspector, I fully understand the importance of impartiality. As employees of the police, we have a duty to treat every person that we meet in a fair and unbiased manner. This doesn't just apply to the public, but also to our own staff members. As leaders within the police force, it's important that inspectors can operate in an impartial manner. Only by treating everyone fairly, can we gain the respect of the public and our colleagues. The police are there to protect everyone, and not just certain members of the community. For this reason, it's essential that we can demonstrate impartiality in all areas of our work.*

*Personally, I am someone who believes strongly in this. I am of the belief that everyone deserves to be treated in a fair and equal manner, and am always ready to challenge discrimination or bias when I see it. My rule is to treat others as you would like to be treated, and I exercise this view in all areas of my life.*

**Q2. In 200 words or less, tell us why public service is important to you.**

## How to Answer

As you can see, this question takes a slightly different approach, questioning your personal opinion, rather than asking about how it relates to the job. That being said, your answer should still be highly similar to the previous, in that it needs to cover both your own viewpoint and your knowledge of why this is important for the police. Take a look at the sample response below for an indication of how to answer.

## Sample Response

*Public service is really important to me. I believe strongly that the best way for society to function is to have services such as the police protecting the interests of the public. It's important to have organisations such as the police in place, to provide security and safety for the general public. Skills such as customer service and communication, as well as being able to understand the differing needs of different communities, are integral in this. This is especially important for inspectors, who are tasked with organising investigations and planning community policing projects. Thus, it's essential that you have a full understanding of the requirements of each community, and how inspectors can use good public service to meet these requirements.*

*As a professional, I have spent the majority of my career in customer service roles, therefore I have a great deal of experience in managing related situations. I firmly believe that I can transfer these skills into the role of police inspector.*

Now that you've looked at the above two responses, have a go at completing your own answers to the next few practice questions.

**Q3. In 200 words or less, what does the term 'transparency' mean to you, and why do you think it's an important quality for police inspectors to have?**

Your Response

**Q4. In 200 words or less, explain to us why integrity is important for police inspectors, and how this quality applies to you.**

Your Response

**Q5. In 200 words or less, explain the importance of leadership when working as a police inspector, and what the term 'leadership' means to you.**

Your Response

**Q6. In 200 words or less, explain the role of organisation when working as a police inspector, and how this quality applies to you.**

Your Response

Before we move onto the next section, take a look over the following top tips for completing a fantastic application form!

## FINAL TIPS FOR COMPLETING A SUCCESSFUL APPLICATION FORM

Whilst some of the following tips have already been provided within this section, it is important that we provide them again. Your success very much depends on your ability to do the following:

- Read the application form and the guidance notes at least twice before you complete it;

- If possible, photocopy the application form and complete a draft copy first. This will allow you to make any errors or mistakes without being penalised;

- Obtain a copy of the core competencies and have them at your side when completing the form;

- Take your time when completing the form and set aside plenty of time for each question. We recommend that you spend five evenings completing the application form breaking it down into manageable portions. This will allow you to maintain high levels of concentration;

- Be honest when completing the form and if you are unsure about anything contact the Police Service for confirmation;

- Try not to make any spelling or grammar errors. You WILL lose marks for poor spelling, grammar and punctuation;

- Try to use keywords and phrases in your responses to the assessable questions that are relevant to the core competencies;

- Try to submit the form well before the closing date;

- If your form is unsuccessful ask for feedback, if available. It is important that you learn from your mistakes.


## WHAT HAPPENS AFTER I HAVE SENT OFF MY APPLICATION FORM?

Once you have completed and sent off your application form, there will be a wait period before you find out whether or not you have been successful. Then, you'll find out their decision via email.

Regardless of the wait, it is crucial that you start preparing for the next stages even before you receive your result. By starting your preparation early you will effectively be giving yourself a 2-3 week advantage over the other applicants. 99% of applicants will wait to receive their result before they start to prepare. This is where you can gain an advantage.

The next stage in the process is a telephone interview.

# THE TELEPHONE
# INTERVIEW

As you can imagine, the police inspector application process is extremely popular. You can guarantee that they will have hundreds upon hundreds of applicants for the role. This means an awful lot of applications to sift through. Naturally, the police can't send through every single person who applies – as there simply wouldn't be room. With this in mind, it's important that they can sift out candidates who might not be right for the role. A telephone interview is far more cost-effective and efficient than screening hundreds of applicants at an assessment day. It should also be noted that instead of a telephone interview, you may also be asked to take a Skype interview. However, the skills utilised in this will be more or less the same, so all of our tips from this chapter will still apply – regardless of the format.

In essence, a telephone interview is a sifting process. Unfortunately, due to this, many candidates don't really take telephone interviews particularly seriously. They want to get to the next stage as quickly as possible, and start readying themselves for the all-important face-to-face interview. This is a huge mistake. If you want to reach the next stage, you need to fully prepare for the telephone interview.

## What does the police inspector telephone interview focus on?

The police inspector telephone interview is largely focused around competency-based questions, and gauging your motivation for working as an inspector. This means that your interview will actually be fairly similar to what you will experience in the actual physical interview stage, or indeed any interview for that matter. While you will be expected to have a good knowledge of the role, and the core competencies, there won't be any questions particular to 'phone interviews' that you have to watch out for.

That being said, be careful. Due to the fact that they aren't physically face-to-face with the interviewers, many people relax too much. They answer the phone while lying in bed, or watching TV. This is a HUGE mistake. In order to do your best at a phone interview, you need to find a quiet place where you can sit, listen and respond calmly to the questions being asked. Numerous studies have shown that your body language can dramatically affect your phone persona. In order to ensure you give the best impression to the interviewer, you need to be in the right place to do it.

During a telephone interview, the employer will not really be able to assess your 'likeability' factor, or whether you will fit into their team and organisation. However, a telephone interview is perfect for assessing whether or not you have the right skills, qualities and experiences for the job. Furthermore, while an application form is a great way of assessing people, it doesn't involve any physical interaction with the person writing it. This can make it very difficult for assessors to ascertain whether that person is suitable.

In order to be successful in your phone interview, or indeed any interview, you need to be able to demonstrate the core competencies through clear and relevant examples. Below, we have listed a number of sample questions that you could expect from the inspector phone interview, along with descriptions on how to answer these. This should help you to understand how you can use the competencies in your own responses to the questions.

To further aid you, make sure you use the **STAR method**:

The **STAR** method works most effectively when preparing responses to situational type interview questions. It ensures that your responses to the interview questions follow a concise and logical sequence and makes sure that you cover every possible area.

**S**ituation – At the commencement of your response, explain what the situation was and who else was involved. This will be a relatively comprehensive explanation so that the interviewer fully understands what it is you are trying to explain.

**T**ask – Explain what the task was. This will basically be an explanation of what had to be done and by whom.

**A**ction – Next, move on and explain what action you specifically took, and also what action other people took.

**R**esult – Finally, explain what the result was following your actions. It is important to make sure that the result was positive as a direct result of your actions.

Using this method not only shows your thought process for each response, but it allows you to take the time and think carefully about each step in the process of your response.

The competency-based questions from the application form are a great starting point to help you prepare for the telephone interview questions.

Remember that since this interview effectively takes the form of a conversation, you will likely be asked to expand on specific points.

## Example Questions

Below, we have laid out a typical series of police inspector telephone interview questions, along with some tips on how to answer them. Later in this guide, we'll provide you with a dedicated interview chapter, where we provide you with full sample responses to all of the below questions, and many more.

### Q1. Could you tell me about why you have applied for the role of a Police Inspector?

One of the aims of the telephone interview is for the police to gauge your interest in the role. This doesn't have to be a lengthy response, just make sure that a) you convey a genuine interest and give good, logical reasons for wanting to work there, and b) match your response with what was put on the application form. In order to ensure you do this, print off your application form prior to sending it off, and then have a copy next to you when you are speaking to the interviewer.

Remember to keep your answer sensible. For example, an answer that lists, 'I want to drive around in a car with flashing lights' or 'I like the uniform' as reasons for wanting to work as a police inspector is unlikely to impress the interviewer. Keep your answer short, concise and realistic. Try to show the interviewer an awareness of current events that the police are dealing with. A good answer to this question will bring up important issues such as leadership, making a difference to the community and safeguarding the public.

Have a go at answering this for yourself, in the textbox on the next page.

**Q2. What do you know about the role of police inspector, and what is it about this role specifically that attracts you?**

In this question, the interviewer is looking for confirmation that you understand the requirements of the role, and some indication that you have performed research into exactly what the role involves. Working as a police inspector is often difficult and stressful, and you will be under large amounts of pressure.

Therefore, it's really important that you know exactly what you are applying for. If you have not bothered to research the position by this point, then it is likely that you are not the type of person that the police want working for them. You can also impress the interviewer by showing knowledge of other roles within the organisation, and highlighting why the role you have chosen is the best fit for you.

Have a go at answering this for yourself, in the textbox on the next page.

**Q3. Can you elaborate more on why you think this role would suit you?**

This is a great question, as it allows you to elaborate upon and go into detail about the skills you have introduced in your previous answers. Later in the interview, you can give specific detailed examples of how you match the competencies. Here, you should give a brief outline of examples of when you have used your skillset to your advantage, and how you believe it could be used when working for the police.

Have a go at answering this for yourself, in the textbox on the next page.

**Q4. What is your biggest weakness?**

When answering this question, be careful. The worst answer that you can give here is, 'I don't have any weaknesses'. This will show a lack of self-awareness to the interviewer. They need to see that you are someone who recognises that there are always improvements to be made, and that you believe the police are the best organisation to help you do that. Obviously, don't reel off a big list of weaknesses here. The key is to pick one weakness, and try to put a positive spin on it. For example, you could tell the interviewer that you sometimes struggle to delegate work, because you are a perfectionist. As long as you make sure to tell the interviewer that you are working on solving this issue, this will show them that you are someone who prioritises attention to detail and good work.

Have a go at answering this for yourself, in the textbox on the next page.

**Q5. Give me an example of a time when you have had to demonstrate good customer service. How did you go about doing this?**

This is a good example of a competency-based question. Using the STAR approach, as outlined in the previous chapter, give a problem-solution-resolution answer to this question. Make sure you tell the interviewer in clear detail about how the problem was fixed as a result of your actions, and you could even incorporate what you learned from the experience.

Have a go at answering this for yourself, in the textbox on the next page.

### Q6. Give me an example of a time when you have faced criticism. How did you deal with this?

When working as a police inspector, you will be operating under highly pressurised conditions. Therefore, it's vital that you are someone who is able to use criticism constructively, in order to improve yourself. Everyone makes mistakes, the key is to learn from your mistakes and produce better results next time. If you can show the interviewer that you recognise this, you will stand a greater chance of passing the interview.

Finish your example by showing the interviewer how your actions are now much better, and that you have improved yourself. Not only does this show an ability to learn and better yourself, but it also displays the key expectation of teamwork.

Have a go at answering this for yourself, in the textbox on the next page.

**Q7. Give me an example of a time when you have had to work as part of a team to solve a problem.**

In this question, you are being asked to demonstrate your teamworking ability. Part of working as a member of a team also involves using some of the other behaviours that the police are looking for, such as: good communication and organisation. Finally, this question is indirectly questioning your own composure and analytical abilities, as the question is specifically referring to the way in which **your** actions benefitted the team. Once again, make sure you use the STAR method to show how you went about solving the issue.

Have a go at answering this for yourself, in the textbox on the next page.

**Q8. Give me an example of a time when you have had to use your analytical skills to solve a problem.**

This question focuses specifically around your analytical ability, but could also involve attention to detail and accuracy. Along with this, in order to solve difficult problems, you will have to take an organised and efficient approach. Analytical thinking is absolutely key to working as a police inspector, and will be a frequent part of your daily professional life. In your answer, you should show a willingness to take initiative, and emphasise your attention to detail.

Have a go at answering this for yourself, in the textbox on the next page.

## Q9. Give me an example of a time when you have taken a flexible approach to solving problems.

This question is essentially asking you to demonstrate that you are someone who is able to adapt their priorities according to the seriousness of the problem that you are dealing with. When you are working as a police inspector, you might be juggling a range of different projects at once. Thus, you need to have a flexible and adaptable approach. You must be able to prioritise issues according to their current status, rather than just the order in which you started working on them.

In the interview chapter of this guide, you will find sample responses to the above and many more interview questions. Below, we've included a list of top general tips for passing a phone interview.

### 10 important tips for passing any telephone interview:

### Tip Number 1

When you have a date for your telephone interview, immediately place it in your diary. You should then start preparing immediately for it. Most people prepare the night before the telephone interview, which is not particularly good practice! You have a lot of work to do, so the sooner you start the better. The areas that you need to work on are:

- How you communicate on the telephone;

- Researching the role you are applying for (you can do this by getting a copy of the job description or person specification).

### Tip Number 2

Before the telephone interview commences, make sure that:

- Your telephone is fully charged (if using a mobile phone);

- You are in an area that has a good reception (if using a mobile telephone);

- You will not be disturbed by anyone or anything.

### Tip Number 3

When the police call you to undertake the telephone interview, make sure you speak clearly and concisely.

Although the interviewer cannot see you, they will form an opinion of how you communicate. Communicating effectively includes:

- Speaking clearly and concisely;

- Being professional at all times;

- Avoiding the use of abbreviations or slang;

- Listening to what the interviewer has to say and answering the questions appropriately.

## Tip Number 4

It is far better to be seated comfortably in a quiet room away from any distractions during the telephone interview. Some people prefer to stand up and walk around; however, if you do this you are likely to breathe heavily during the interview, which may be distracting to the interviewer.

## Tip Number 5

Make sure you have a copy of your application form in front of you during the telephone interview. It is also advisable that you have a copy of your CV. This way, if the interviewer asks you questions about your previous employment or qualification dates, then you will have the information to hand.

## Tip Number 6

Have a pen and piece of paper in front of you so that you can write down notes and even briefly write down any questions they put to you, so that you can refer back to them during questioning.

## Tip Number 7

It's useful to have a glass of water to hand during a phone interview (but move the phone away from your mouth when you swallow). You will be doing a lot of talking and you don't want your mouth to dry up at a crucial moment during the telephone interview.

## Tip Number 8

Be sure to smile when speaking during the telephone interview. You would be amazed at the difference it makes to your tone of voice. Even though they cannot see you, they will hear a positive vibe in your voice if you smile whilst you speak!

### Tip Number 9

During a face-to-face interview, you interact with the interviewer by nodding your head and showing facial expressions. Obviously you cannot do this during a telephone interview. Therefore, you have to show that you are paying attention by using small phrases and communicational confirmations such as "OK", "uh-huh", "I see", "I understand", "yes" or similar quotes/phrases.

### Tip Number 10

A large part of the telephone interview assessment will be how you communicate. Communicating effectively is not just about how you speak, it's also about how you listen. Listen to what the interviewer has to say and engage with them positively. Do not come across as monotone, boring or disinterested. Always be positive.

Now, let's move onto the assessment centre!

# THE POLICE INSPECTOR ASSESSMENT CENTRE

If you pass the telephone interview, then you will be invited to attend the direct entry police inspector assessment centre. This consists of a series of days spent at a testing centre, taking part in various activities and tests, which will enable the police to establish your suitability for the course.

The tests that you will take at the assessment centre are extremely difficult. Unlike most assessment centres, which take place over just 1 day, the inspector assessment centre is intentionally held over 2 or 3 days – to enable extra testing of the candidates. Remember, places on the direct entry course are extremely exclusive, and only the very best candidates will progress.

**What tests will I have to take?**

In total, you will need to take 7 exercises over the course of the assessment centre. The assessment centre will take place over 3 days, and will usually consist of the following timetable:

• **Day 1.** Registration;

• **Day 2**. A full day of exercises;

• **Day 3**. A half day of exercises.


The tests will generally consist of the following:

• An event briefing exercise;

• An in-tray exercise (written);

• A performance management task;

• A values assessment;

• A presentation;

• Cognitive ability tests;

• An interview.

The tests are designed to reflect the work that real police inspectors will need to do, on a daily basis. This is particularly true for the event briefing, in-tray, performance management and values exercises. Having said that, not all of the tests will be based around real police scenarios. Some of the tests are simply there to test you on the necessary skills, rather than on your knowledge of policing. However, all of the tests have been designed around the core competencies required for the police, and the key behaviours that are connected with these.

## How Will I Be Assessed?

For each exercise, you will be scored based on how well you meet the competencies, and how well you completed the tasks. You will be assessed by a number of different individuals, both inside and outside of the police force. The assessors from within the police force will consist of high-ranking officers, who are working at the level of inspector, superintendent and above. The assessors from outside the force will consist of individuals who are involved in the selection of senior level employees, both in the public and private sectors. These individuals will be highly experienced in judging whether an applicant is suitable for the position.

Before we move onto the exercises, refer back to page 16 for the core competencies.

Once you've looked over the competencies again, we can get started with looking at the actual tests that you will take.

# The Assessment Centre Tests

**Please note, the order of these tests is subjective, and you may be asked to take the tests in a different order to the way in which they are listed here. Furthermore, please note that these tests are NOT an exact replica of what you will face in the assessment centre. We have designed these tests to help you practice the skills required for passing the Inspector process, and they are not designed to be used as a replacement for the test itself.**

## Event Briefing

The first exercise is an Event Briefing. The Event Briefing takes part in two stages:

- The preparation phase;
- The role play phase.

During the first part of the Event Briefing, you will be given a pack of information about a fictional scenario. You will then be given 40 minutes to read through this information pack, and prepare.

During the second part of the Event Briefing, you will be asked to give a briefing on the materials to two assessors and a role play actor, based on how you plan to deal with the events discussed in the information pack. The second part of the Event Briefing can also be broken down into two stages, which are as follows:

Stage 1: You'll have 10 minutes to brief the individuals within the room about the scenario, and your solutions to it.

Stage 2: You'll have 15 minutes to answer questions from the assessors and role play actor, based on the briefing.

### What is the purpose of the Event Briefing?

As mentioned, the assessment centre exercises are designed to test you on how well you can deal with common scenarios you'll face in your career. As a police inspector, you can expect to be delivering very regular briefings. You won't just need to give briefings to your staff – informing them on how you plan to deal with a particular issue, but also to your superiors, who will be working to determine whether you have taken the correct course of action. For this reason, an event briefing is a perfect way to test your skills.

So, what skills are being tested here? Let's find out.

### What does the Event Briefing show?

Giving a briefing to a room full of people is no easy task. Regardless of the profession in which you find yourself, public speaking is difficult even for the best for us. As mentioned, police inspectors will need to give regular briefings to both their staff and their superiors. So, what does the event briefing show? Let's look at some of the qualities that are being assessed here:

**Communication.** The Event Briefing will give the assessors a very accurate idea of how good your communication skills are. Naturally, if you are addressing a room full of people, then your communication will need to be top notch. The ideas that you present must be clear and logical, and backed up by supportive evidence. By the end of your briefing, the assessors should be in no doubt about the situation itself, and must have a general idea (at the very least) of how you plan to resolve it. Areas such as keeping eye contact, speaking slowly and clearly, using hand movements and affirmative gestures, will all go a long way to helping you do this.

**Attention to detail.** Attention to detail is extremely important in the Event Briefing, and in your work as a police inspector. Given that you have 40 minutes to read through the briefing pack, the assessors will expect you to have learned the source material down to the most minute of details. It is your job to decide which of these details is the most fundamental, but you will need to ensure that you address all of the main points. Likewise, you do not want to be in a position where the assessors are asking you questions to which you don't know the answers! This could be highly embarrassing, and strongly detract from your score.

**Decision-making.** The Event Briefing will also test your decision-making skills. Since you are providing a briefing to the assessors, you need to provide them with solutions to the problems listed in the scenario. This means that you need to make educated and logical decisions, based on what you have read. Your decisions will be weighed up by the assessors, and called into question during the second stage of the briefing exercise.

Now that we've looked at the above, let's have a go at a sample exercise:

### Sample Event Briefing Exercise

As mentioned, the Event Briefing exercise will give you 40 minutes' worth of materials to look through. Obviously, we can't provide you with something that extensive, however we can provide you with some tests which help you to practice the same skills.

Take a look at the below scenario:

> You are the customer services officer for a fictitious retail centre. Your manager has asked you to compile a report based on a new pub that is being opened in the centre. Your manager is meeting with the pub owners in a few days' time to discuss a few issues and he wants you to write a report based on the information provided. The pub owners have requested that the pub is open to serve alcohol beverages in the centre from 11am until 11pm.

Here is a survey sheet that tells you that, on the whole, the general public and staff are not happy with the idea of a pub being opened in the shopping centre because of perceived antisocial behavioural problems, including littering and rowdiness.

## SURVEY SHEET

The following information has been taken from a survey that was conducted amongst 100 members of public who regularly shop at the centre and 30 employees who work at the centre.

- 60% of the general public and 80% of employees felt that the opening of a pub in the centre would increase littering;

- 80% of the general public and 60% of employees thought that rowdiness in the centre would increase as a result of the pub opening;

- 10% of the general public and 10% of employees thought that the opening of the pub would be a good idea.

On the following page, there is an example of how the report could be written. There are many different recommendations that could have been made.

You should consider the information you have gathered and make the recommendation(s) you consider to be the best for those circumstances.

Remember: recommendations are suggestions for actions or changes. They should be specific rather than general. It is important that you answer the question and state what your main findings and recommendations are.

Below we've listed a sample response to the above. Remember that you won't need to write a response out to the assessors, as you'll be actually standing there talking to them, but the below should hopefully give you some idea of how to approach the scenario:

*Dear Sir,*

*Please find detailed my findings and recommendations in relation to the new pub as requested. The survey conducted took into the consideration the views and opinions of 100 members of the public and 30 members of staff who work at the centre. Whilst a small proportion of staff and public (10%) felt that the opening of the pub would be a good idea, the majority of people surveyed felt that there would be problems with antisocial behaviour, littering and rowdiness.*

*Having taken into consideration all of the information provided, I wish to make the following recommendations: The level of customer service that the centre currently provides is high and it is important that this is maintained. It is important to take into consideration the views and opinions of our customers and staff and to see things from their point of view. I believe that there would be a high risk involved if we were to allow the pub to serve alcoholic beverages from 11am until 11pm and that problems with anti-social behaviour could develop.*

*We have a responsibility to protect the public and to ensure that they are safe whilst in the centre. While it is important to initially obtain the views of the pub owners, I recommend that the pub is only permitted to serve alcoholic beverages from 11am until 1pm and from 5pm until 7pm in order to reduce the risk of the above problems developing.*

*I have recommended this course of action, as I believe it is in the best interests of the centre, its staff and more importantly our valued customers. This alternative course of action would be for a trial period only and providing there are no problems with anti-social behaviour, littering or rowdiness we could look to review the opening hours with a view to extending them. I am prepared to take full responsibility for monitoring the situation once the pub has been opened. I will keep you updated on progress.*

Now that you have read the sample response, take a look at the following 4 step approach that you can use during the briefing exercise. These tips specifically apply during the 40 minute preparation period:

**Step 1** – Read the information provided in the exercise as quickly and accurately as possible. Remember that while you have 40 minutes to read through the information, you also need to come up with solutions, and find a way to memorise the information. Therefore, you don't want to spend too long just reading through it all.

**Step 2** – Extract relevant information from irrelevant information. When you read the information provided in the briefing pack, you will notice that some of the information is of no significance. Establish which information is relevant, and then use this when you brief the assessors.

**Step 3** – Decide what recommendations you are going to suggest, or what actions you are going to take. One of the police inspector core competencies is that of problem solving. You must come up with suitable recommendations. Do not 'sit on the fence', but rather provide a logical solution to the problem.

**Step 4** – Ensure that the solutions you have produced, line up with the core competencies/behavioural expectations. Every single solution that you produce must be in line with the police values. Suggestions which counteract these values, will detract from your marks.

You will notice that the 4 step approach is easy to follow. Therefore we strongly suggest that you learn it and use it during the practice exercises provided later on in this section.

To begin with, let's go back to the sample response that we provided in the first exercise and we will explain how to implement the 4 step approach:

**Step 1** requires you to read the information quickly and accurately. We recommend reading through it two times. The first time, read through the entire document thoroughly, making sure you pay attention to everything. The second time, try and read through it, but isolate the key/essential points. As you do this, you can already start to form links between what is essential, and how these relate to the core competencies.

**Step 2** requires you to extract relevant information from irrelevant information. In order to demonstrate what is relevant, we have bolded the key points below:

**You are the customer services officer** for a fictitious retail centre. Your manager has asked you to compile a report based on a **new pub that is being opened in the centre.**

Your manager is meeting with the pub owners in a few days' time to discuss a few issues and he wants you to write a report based on the information provided. **The pub owners have requested that the pub is open to serve alcohol beverages in the centre from 11am until 11pm.**

Here is a survey sheet that tells you that, on the whole, **the general public and staff are not happy with the idea of a pub being opened in the shopping centre** because of perceived antisocial behavioural problems, littering and rowdiness.

Remember: recommendations are suggestions for actions or changes. They should be specific rather than general. It is important that you answer the question and state what your main findings and recommendations are.

So, why are the key points that we underlined relevant? Allow us to explain:

**You are the customer services officer.**

Because you will have already read the Welcome Pack prior to attending the assessment centre and in particular your duties and responsibilities within it, you will have noticed that it is your job to provide a high level of service. Therefore the briefing needs to cater for everyone's needs. In relation to this particular situation, you must provide a solution that caters for the needs of the pub owners, the centre and also the members of public and employees.

**New pub that is being opened in the centre.**

The information you have been provided with tells you clearly that a new pub is opening in the centre. Therefore, the pub needs to operate as a business and by doing so it needs to serve alcoholic beverages. Despite the fact that the majority of people surveyed are against the pub opening, the pub still needs to function as a business. Bear this in mind when detailing your recommendations.

**The pub owners have requested that the pub is open to serve alcohol beverages in the centre from 11am until 11pm.**

The pub owners have quite rightly requested that they open from 11am until 11pm and serve alcoholic beverages throughout this period. However, you still need to provide a high level of service to everyone. Therefore, you may decide to recommend a reduced opening time for a trial period only. Always look for the obvious solution to the problem.

**The general public and staff are not happy with the idea of a pub being opened in the shopping centre.**

Because the general public and staff are not happy with the idea of a pub opening in the centre, you will need to take this into account when constructing your response.

During **Step 3**, you will need to come up with your recommendations. Remember that as an inspector, you will need to solve problems based on the information and facts provided. In this particular case, we have decided to offer a solution that meets the needs of all parties concerned – reduced opening times for a trial period with a view to extending them if all goes well. When creating your report do not be afraid to come up with sensible recommendations or solutions.

During **Step 4** you will check that your solutions match with the core competencies. Go through the solution to each problem, and ensure that it matches with at least one of the core behavioural expectations/ values. If there is any potential clash, then it's likely that there is a problem with your solution. Although the solutions might be a little more difficult to come up with; matching them with the core competencies should be fairly simple. It's easy to see whether a solution contradicts one of the core expectations, as this is mostly just common sense.

The final extra step in delivering your briefing, is to use keywords and phrases when writing your response, which are relevant to the core competencies and key behaviours being assessed. The following are sentences and phrases that we used whilst creating the report, which relate to a number of competency and key behavioural areas:

- "The level of customer service that the centre currently provides is high and it is important that this is maintained" – relates to public service;

- "It is important to take into consideration the views and opinions of our customers and staff and to see things from their point of view" – relates to public service;

- "I believe that there would be a high risk involved if we were to allow the pub to serve alcoholic beverages from 11am until 11pm and that problems with antisocial behaviour could develop" – relates to decision making and professionalism;

- "We have a responsibility to protect the public and to ensure that they are safe whilst in the centre" – relates to professionalism and public service;

- "While it is important to initially obtain the views of the pub owners, I recommend that the pub is only permitted to serve alcoholic beverages from 11am until 1pm and from 5pm until 7pm in order to reduce the risk of the above problems developing" – relates to openness to change and decision making;

- "I have recommended this course of action, as I believe it is in the best interests of the centre, its staff and more importantly our valued customers" – relates to public service;

- "This alternative course of action would be for a trial period only and providing there are no problems with antisocial behaviour, littering or rowdiness we could look to review the opening hours with a view to extending them" – relates to openness to change and decision making;

- "I am prepared to take full responsibility for monitoring the situation once the pub has been opened" – relates to professionalism.

Before you move onto the next exercise, here are some brief final tips to help you with your briefing:

## Important Tips to Help With Your Briefing

- Remember that you are being assessed based on your ability to communicate effectively. This means delivering a briefing that is concise, relevant, easy-to-read and free from errors;

- Make sure you answer the question, and actually provide solutions to the problem that is listed;

- Use keywords and phrases from the core competencies. This is how the police will assess you;

- Do not spend too much time reading the information and documentation provided. Try to balance out your reading, with finding solutions.

## Values Exercise

Along with the Event Briefing, you will also be required to take a Values Exercise. This is a highly similar task to the Event Briefing, but is far shorter in length. During the Values Exercise, you will again have to read through information about a fictional scenario, before briefing the assessors on your plan of action/resolutions. You'll have just 15 minutes to read through the materials, 8 minutes to deliver your briefing, and 12 minutes for taking questions from the assessors. The Values Exercise will aim to test you on different competencies to those used during the event briefing exercise, but many of the same competencies will still apply. That is to say, you will still need to demonstrate skills such as communication, problem solving and professionalism – but, the scenario that you will encounter in this exercise is more likely to challenge you based on your knowledge of the police values, such as public service and integrity.

## Written In-Tray Exercise

The next exercise that you will need to take, is a Written In-Tray Exercise. An in-tray exercise is a paper-based simulation, which is used to assess your organisational and problem-solving skills. You'll be presented with a number of related tasks, such as emails, complaints or reports, and required to place them into an acceptable order/deal with them in a set manner. The assessors will judge based on how well you prioritise the tasks, and work through them in an efficient manner. The exercise takes 2 hours to complete. You'll be provided with a set of documents, listing the tasks that need to be completed, and you will also be provided with a laptop – upon which you can write your responses to the tasks. The laptops will utilise the latest version of Microsoft Word, meaning it's beneficial to familiarise yourself with this software beforehand.

### How does the In-Tray Exercise relate to the role?

As you know, organisation is a key element of working as a police inspector. Police inspectors will have a huge number of things to deal with each and every single day, meaning that you will often be swamped with different tasks. The in-tray exercise is designed to assess how well you can deal with this. It is an attempt to simulate a specific situation. Typically, you play the part of the employee who has come in either first thing in the morning or to a first day in a job, and there is a list of activities and events that you need to tackle.

You'll normally be given some information about the company and a calendar, in order to help you.

The in-tray exercise may also contain:

• Letters of complaint;

- General letters/correspondence;
- Memos;
- Emails;
- Notes.

During an in-tray exercise test, the assessors are looking for:

- Your ability to process information;
- Your capacity for analysing problems and future repercussions;
- How you make decisions under pressure and prioritise effectively;
- Your creativity;
- How you assess potential problems;
- How effective you are at implementing solutions;
- How you manage time effectively;
- How you deal with people tactfully;
- Your ability to delegate some tasks;
- Your ability to consider the wider implications for the organisation;
- How you negotiate and/or influence others.

## Sample In-Tray Exercise

Using the above information, have a go at the following very simple example:

Put a '1' by the first activity you would undertake and '2' by the second, until you have covered all the activities. For the purposes of this exercise, try to explain your reasoning for each selection.

| Item 1 | Issue left on desk - a message left by the Head asking you to proofread the final copy of the new school prospectus that is due for the printers. This needs to be ready for distribution at the start of the new term. | |
|---|---|---|
| Item 2 | Issue on desk – draft copy of a newsletter to go out to parents today about an event next week – the manuscript needs attention before passing to the Admin office. | |
| Item 3 | Fax – arrived through at 08:25 from Social Services about a child protection issue with regards to a student in year 2, which has arisen during the last couple of days. Social Services want an urgent response. | |
| Item 4 | Phone call comes in from a supply teacher that you engaged to cover the Head's teaching duties –"Sorry, can't come in, I'm off sick." | |
| Item 5 | Phone message from the finance office to remind the Head that the budget return is overdue and is needed by 12 noon today. | |
| Item 6 | The head has left you his/her password and has asked that you make sure that the Head Teacher inbox is emptied of emails every day, and that each one is dealt with on the day it comes in. The mail box is currently showing 30 messages. | |

| Item 7 | Following a knock at the door, the caretaker enters to report on a serious broken glass problem in a classroom, as a result of vandalism the previous evening. | |
|--------|---|---|
| Item 8 | You hear shouting in the corridor - it sounds like a parent that wants to speak with the Head. They sound angry. | |
| Item 9 | The post contains a letter of resignation from a Learning Assistant who cites bullying by the class teacher with whom she normally works. She is at work this morning. | |
| Item 10 | In the post is an offer of free trips to a summer school for disadvantaged year 1 children - but applications need to be in immediately. | |
| Item 11 | The door opens and in comes Andy Cappel, a local authority officer who was just passing by, and thought he would drop in to see how the refurbishments on the school are going. | |

Hopefully, this exercise wasn't too hard. It is a fairly simple and straightforward version of an in-tray activity. Did you notice that some of the items were more urgent than others, and that some demanded a more immediate response?

Remember that just because someone is demanding a quick response, it does not mean that you have to give it to them. There are no right or wrong answers to this, as long as you justify every stage.

Below is an example of how to answer this question:

1. **Item 3.** This has warnings all over it. 'Child protection, social services' connotes that there could be a child in danger, and if it were to come to court, you would need to account for the reason that you delayed action. Therefore, you should act immediately.

2. **Item 7.** Broken glass requires immediate attention (health and

safety) and the police would need to be called regarding the vandalism.

3. **Item 8.** Ask the parent to take a seat in reception, and offer them a drink. Often when irate people wait for a few minutes their anger dissipates - but I would only leave this parent for a few minutes at most.

4. **Item 9.** Ask the teacher concerned to come to your office, and tell them that you would like to speak with them at break time. You could then excuse them from their duties for the morning, as there could be an investigation later in the day. Depending on the severity of the accusation, you could send them home and tell them that you will be in touch. Bullying is a very serious accusation, and must be dealt with appropriately.

5. **Item 4.** To deal with the teaching issue, contact reception and ask them to give you a list of teachers who are free during this period. You could then arrange for one of these teachers to take a break later in the day, so that they can cover the head's teaching duties.

6. **Item 2.** The newsletter must go out today, or parents will have insufficient notice to attend the event. It should only take a moment to read through, and this task could even be delegated.

7. **Item 11.** Arrange for Mr Cappel to come in at a later date in the week.

8. **Item 5.** Ring the finance office and see whether there is any leeway on the budget timetable. If there isn't, deal with it here and then send it off.

9. **Item 1.** It is not clear whether this is particularly important, but it could be done in the evening and then sent to the printers tomorrow.

10. **Item 6.** Emails are answered quickest in one sitting, and this could be done when you have a free period later in the day.

11. **Item 10.** This is a nice gesture but requires some thought. You will need to involve teachers and change timetables, and this could cause some problems if you rush it.

There are some items that could be done in parallel, some that could have been pushed even further down the list (such as item 11), some you need to make assumptions about (item 4), and some you do not know how complex the situation might be (item 8). This is why you need to justify and explain your actions.

An important point to consider is that there are very few right or wrong answers in these lists. There could be lengthy debates over whether a certain activity should be number 14 or 15, and some of this might even relate to any real life experiences that you have had.

For example, if you have had an experience where dealing with a complaint has gone terribly wrong, then you might be inclined to give it more priority.

Similarly, if you found that the way in which you handled the issue last time was perfect, then you might place it lower down the list since you'll feel that you know how to handle it. The reason that you need to justify your selection is that this will help the assessor to see that you are someone who understands the main principles of prioritising, and that you are someone who is able to justify their decisions with clear and logical reasoning.

That said, there are still key activities that should always come within the top third, then a medium set, and finally a low priority set. Arranging the activities into these three groups can make the in-tray exercise far more manageable. What you name the groups is entirely up to you, but it should be something similar to: High Priority, Medium Priority and Low Priority.

## How to ensure maximum results

The first thing you should do when given an in-tray exercise is to read through all of the paper work that you have been given. Look at the company background, or consider any information that is important to the decisions you are about to make. For example, in the school scenario, the head teacher has a duty of care towards both the children and staff. Remember that any background information provided to you, has been provided for a reason. If you are told that severe rain is forecast, then this is an important point that you will be expected to take into consideration.

If you are provided with an organisational chart, pay attention to who is performing which job. This can make a difference to how you respond to certain situations. You should also take note of specific dates. A complaint letter that is four days old may become suddenly more urgent. In our school example, you are given the date so that you can judge where you are in relation to particular items (such as Item 1).

You also need to make sure that you follow the written instructions carefully. Some exercises will just ask you to place the activities in order, whereas others will ask you to complete a diary. Some may ask you to provide written explanations for every decision that you make, and some might ask you to start drafting replies to the respondents or write what you would actually do in each situation.

It's also important to have a clear idea of the time limit, to ensure that you allocate sufficient time for each part of the task. Finally, make a rough plan and note how you are going to undertake the exercise. Read through all of the examples, and make notes or highlight certain words that you need to remember.

Maximise your chances of scoring highly by making sure that you READ EVERYTHING.

Go through the school example again, and put a 1, 2 or 3 in the boxes to indicate whether they should be high, medium or low priority.

Now, look at the situations in each category. For each category, try to place them on the grid below:

|  | Important | Not so important |
|---|---|---|
| **Urgent** | 1 | 2 |
| **Not Urgent** | 3 | 4 |

The key is to balance the items that you think are the most urgent, against their level of importance. For example, if someone is standing in front of you with blood dripping from their hand because of an accident, this would feature in box 1 since it is both urgent and important. It needs to be dealt with now, and fast. However, if a colleague rings and tells you that they are off sick, but they have no classes scheduled for the rest of the week then this is an urgent but not important issue (provided there are no problems with cover).

Therefore, this issue can go into box 2.

Now consider that the colleague who is off sick was meant to be writing a report regarding summer activities, during this week. This is important because it will help the school to raise money, but it is not urgent because it could be written when she comes back to school. Therefore this would feature in section 3.

One mistake that many people make when taking the in-tray exercises is to try and go for the quickest remedies first, in a misguided attempt to knock off five or six activities in the first ten minutes.

Always consider safety first. Anything that puts people in danger, such as an accident, broken glass or an electrical failing needs to be dealt with IMMEDIATELY. Move all of the less urgent requests to the end, such as a request for holiday time off. This leaves you with more time to think through the essential tasks.

**Time Limit**

An in-tray exercise is supposed to put you under pressure. This is because you will need to make decisions as if you were in a working environment, where mistakes can be costly. The key is stay calm, and if there is not sufficient information, you must make educated assumptions. This is a normal part of life, and something that we do every day. You will not be marked down for this unless you fail to consider an important piece of information, or unless your assumption is completely out of the box. For example, if you decide to write to someone who has sent in a complaint, you would be justified in assuming that they are annoyed. Assuming that they are happy and satisfied on the other hand, would be considered strange and unjustified.

If you are asked to give your actions, work through them in a logical order from the most urgent onwards. That way, if you don't reach the end in time, you will have dealt with the main issues. You just need to make sure that the order makes sense before you start writing.

Some activities may be dependent on others, for example your caretaker cannot clear up the glass if he is the staff member off sick. Some activities may take place simultaneously, such as delegating tasks. Give reasons for your decisions wherever you can. Check in the text whether it says that you do not have to do everything else.

Look on the organisation chart, do you have a secretary, assistant, administrator or second in command? What actions could be allocated to them?

## Sample Exercise 2

In some exercises, you will be given a case study file before the exercise, detailing information which you should use to arrange your list.

Below we have provided you with an in-depth case study on the fictional organisation 'BabyMaxPro'. Read all of the information, before answering the in-tray questions.

## Background

You are an employee wanting to secure a general management job at BabyMaxPro. On the following pages you will find a background to the company (such as you would find in a business plan or corporate document) and some additional information in the form of reports and emails.

## Your task

The information presented here will form the background to the various exercises in the assessment centre and will be referred to throughout this book. Read them thoroughly and make notes regarding any aspect you find interesting or where you feel you can impact on this company.

The information given here is completely fictitious and is not based on any real organisation. The information is simulated and therefore you will need to use your own judgement, knowledge and experience to look through the documentation and draw conclusions.

## About BabyMaxPro

BabyMaxPro formed in 1996 when Pharmacists Helen Maxwell and Shaun Maxwell wanted to produce the highest factor skin block for babies on the market. Their son, Callum was born in 1995 with hyper-sensitive skin and they found that none of the proprietary sun blocks on the market at that time both suited his skin and provided the protection he needed.

The name comes from the words 'baby maximum protection' as that is what Helen and Shaun were seeking.

The first creams and lotions were created from their kitchen, but after being featured in a national newspaper, they soon realised that they needed additional premises. BabyMaxPro cream remains a high selling cream with sales of over 2.5 million units around the world, netting the company just under £7 Million per annum. Today the cream is manufactured by Lincoln Pharmaceuticals under contract and the formula remains top secret.

Following the initial success of BabyMaxPro cream, Helen and Shaun developed their baby range to include moisturiser and bath products. These products complement the range and although they are gentle for a baby's skin, they do not contain any specific 'secret' formula. In 1998 Lincoln Pharmaceuticals could not take on this additional range due to their size and the anticipated demand and therefore the bath range is produced by Helix Laboratories. The baby range, although highly profitable, did not achieve the same demand as the original BabyMaxPro cream, and the contract for Helix is up for re-consideration in the next 12 months.

In 2000 Helen Maxwell was asked to judge a competition to find the best female entrepreneur. Although the winner of the competition was Linda Clarke with her 'In a Box' design your own wedding kit, Helen was impressed by another entrant, Kimberly Cresswell who had designed a new feeding cup. Helen felt the feeder cup fitted BabyMaxPro, and so she offered Kimberly a deal on working together with BabyMaxPro, to launch the product under the BabyMaxPro label. Kimberly jumped at the chance and this section of the business now produces all feedingware, including plastic bibs. These are sold under the banner of BabyMaxPro Essentials.

In 2002 at a similar event Helen met fellow judge Paul Dickinson who told her about a new and very different educational toy for very young children that he had designed. Helen made the same offer and the toy, together with five other educational toys, now make up the BabyMaxPro Learning range.

In 2004 the company hit a setback when they tried to launch a clothing line, BabyMaxPro Design. The clothes although beautifully made with natural fabrics were too expensive for the market and could not stand up against cheap imports. It folded after a year, losing the company £3 million in investments, but the two employees on the team were able to be absorbed into the BabyMaxPro Cream and Baby Care team, and there were no redundancies. This is not often discussed, as it caused many problems within the company.

Since 2004 the company has not invested in any new areas, even though they recognise that there has been significant cultural changes in that space of time. Although BabyMaxPro is financially safe, the owners are feeling that it is losing its entrepreneurial image and is in danger of becoming staid and out of touch. BabyMaxPro also has a charitable arm and gives 5% of its profits to infant mortality projects in third world countries.

The ethos of BabyMaxPro has never been to make huge profits. Helen and Shaun care more about providing employment for local people and helping the economy through sustaining jobs. They also want to help other entrepreneurs to find a foothold in the market by offering them an outlet for their inventions through the BabyMaxPro company.

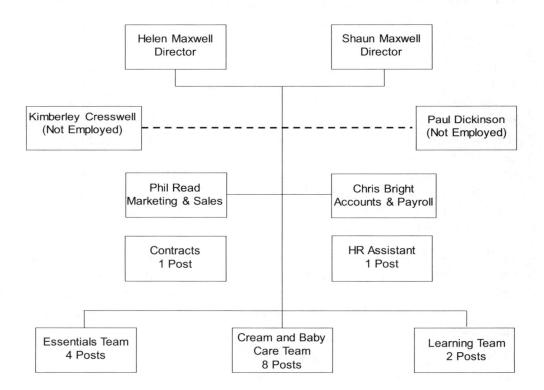

### How we work in BabyMaxPro

At BabyMaxPro we value certain behaviours and work to a set of principles that we believe create a favourable working atmosphere, company growth and sustainability.

Our principles:

## Commercial awareness

We understand that it is important to compete financially and maintain the commercial health of the business. Without sales and our commercial footing BabyMaxPro would not exist. To secure a prosperous future we need to ensure that every employee is business aware and that we are able to deliver a healthy return on investment.

## Collaboration

BabyMaxPro has drawn great strength in working in collaboration with other organisations and entrepreneurs. We also have a history of delivering through great team work. We know that we need to share our capabilities and work together to provide a collective brilliance to compete in the market for tomorrow.

## Innovation

BabyMaxPro is born out of innovation and is known and respected for its creativity. We embrace change and help to nurture new ideas. We actively seek out new ideas from every area of the business, and we are not afraid to invest time in nurturing new talent.

## Respect for everyone

We wish to create an environment where every member of BabyMaxPro feels heard and valued. All staff deserve to work in an environment free from harassment and intimidation; where difference is not only valued but celebrated for the richness it brings to the future of the business.

## Focus on the customer

BabyMaxPro does not exist without customers, and many customers have been loyal to the company since its inception. We aim to honour that loyalty to both our original and new customers by always putting them at the forefront of any business decisions.

## The BabyMaxPro Vision for the Future

Due to steady sales of BabyMaxPro cream we have been fortunate to retain a stronghold in the sun protection area of our business. However, we now need to reduce that risk by strengthening our other brands whilst at the same time, searching for solid innovation.

From this year, all areas of the business will have their own business plans that demonstrate individual growth and sustainability. We will still continue to nurture new ideas and concepts but within an ordered timeframe.

In the coming year, we also need to recapture the essence that made BabyMaxPro an original, innovative company. Therefore we will be looking to expand into at least one new area of business that both complements and grows the BabyMaxPro brand.

## Overview of the Annual Colleague Survey

There was a 100% response rate to this very popular staff feedback tool.

| This year's key finding | Yes | No | Last year's results for comparison | Yes | No |
|---|---|---|---|---|---|
| I have confidence in the direction of the company | 99% | 1% | I have confidence in the direction of the company | 100% | 0% |
| I am happy in my job | 23% | 77% | I am happy in my job | 65% | 35% |
| I feel involved and listened to | 27% | 73% | I feel involved and listened to | 48% | 52% |
| My ideas are discussed in full with the team or my manager | 21% | 79% | My ideas are discussed in full with the team or my manager | 57% | 43% |
| I understand my role fully | 75% | 25% | I understand my role fully | 57% | 43% |
| I am bored in my role | 50% | 50% | I am bored in my role | 20% | 80% |
| I have good opportunities to develop | 20% | 80% | I have good opportunities to develop | 20% | 80% |
| I receive leadership from my line manager | 40% | 60% | I receive leadership from my line manager | 45% | 55% |
| I am proud to be a part of BabyMaxPro | 98% | 2% | I am proud to be a part of BabyMaxPro | 97% | 3% |
| I believe there is a future in BabyMaxPro | 100% | 0% | I believe there is a future in BabyMaxPro | 100% | 0% |

**EMAIL**

Hi,

I have just come back from a new (possible) client, and I am so excited I want to report back. Gareth and Stacy Johns live in Wales and started out making recyclable baby pants from their own sheep's wool. The baby pants are high in lanolin which soothes baby's skin and creates a waterproof barrier that reduces leaks. The pants hold a nappy liner, which is easily disposed, thus cutting down on waste. They have been selling to their dedicated customers for a couple of years with great success and they are creating quite a following, although they are a very small enterprise, possibly only selling in the region of 100 – 150 units per year.

As the farm has been caught in the farming recession they have invested in a new range of babies clothing, again based on the wool from their flock of 'baby faced doll' sheep. The range is very simple: vests, socks, simple cardigans and tights, mainly in cream. The clothing is organic and has been spun in a way that ensures it is exceptionally soft. They are aiming their product at those parents who have an interest in supporting small companies and wish to help the environment.

Gareth and Stacey believe that if they are to take this brand to the next level, they need the backing and support of a larger enterprise. What are your thoughts? Can someone look at this?

Phil Read

**EMAIL**

Hi,

I am sending this from an exhibition at the NEC. I have just met with a company called MeandMama who make buggies and car seats. Briefly, their design is standard, but their safety features and quality are second to none. In a nutshell, they cannot exist much longer in the current marketplace on their own and they are looking for a company to partner with (or even for a buyout) -someone bigger, with established customers. When I told them that BabyMaxPro may be interested they were thrilled and felt that this was just the kind of business they would want to associate their products with. I don't know whether we are interested at all but I am going to ask them to come down to us in about a month to have a conversation as to whether we might be of mutual assistance.

I also wanted to tell you that I have seen a product BabySunSafe that is very similar to BabyMaxPro cream and is selling at half our price.

Chris Bright

**EMAIL**

Hi,

I have been speaking with a number of providers in respect of introducing a leadership programme into the company. Although I have searched the net widely there does not seem to be anyone out there offering exactly what we want for our employees. I think therefore we should be thinking along the lines of commissioning a bespoke programme that fits our principles.

Can you work up some ideas (and possibly some costs) for me to take to the board as soon as possible?

Many thanks,

Mary Stevens

(HR Assistant)

| Item 1 | You have just received an email telling you of industrial action and Lincoln Pharmaceuticals. This is the third case threatened this year. | |
| --- | --- | --- |
| Item 2 | There has been a break-in at the BabyMaxPro offices. Only one computer has gone missing. | |
| Item 3 | You have feedback that your budget figures are incorrect, and there is a board meeting in twenty minutes. | |
| Item 4 | Your assistant (temp) has called in sick with a headache. It is the second time that this has happened in two weeks. | |
| Item 5 | You have an email from an angry customer claiming that BabyMaxPro has caused a rash on their child. | |
| Item 6 | John Brown, one of your staff members, has recently announced that he is about to take his honeymoon! He has been with you for ten years and leaves at midday today. There really ought to be a present for him and his new bride-to-be. | |
| Item 7 | You have just received an email from a journalist in Australia informing you that toys similar to those in the Learning Range have been seen on sale in Australia, under the brand name 'Kismet' – and that company has Paul Dickinson as director. | |
| Item 8 | You have just heard that Stephen Leeming (a guest at the board meeting) has broken down in his car, approximately 15 minutes away from the offices. | |
| Item 9 | Jan Foreman from Today (a top newspaper) rings to request an interview. She would like an interview to do in the weekend supplement and wants to meet you later today. | |

| Item 10 | Jane Pickles comes in to tell you that money has gone missing from the charity fund jar on her desk. She is very upset. | |
| Item 11 | An inspector from the Health and Safety organisation is waiting in reception. He has decided to do a spot check. | |

List the order in which you would go about solving these issues, and justify why.

**TIP:** Don't forget to use the technique that we discussed earlier, sorting the issues into high priority, medium priority, and low priority, along with the urgent-important grid. Use the box below to fill in your answer.

Hopefully, you should now be getting some idea of how to organise your responses. As mentioned, there are no right or wrong answers to these tests, but below we've provided you with an example of how you might look at each of the issues.

**Item 1:** You have just received an email telling you of industrial action at Lincoln Pharmaceuticals. This is the third case threatened this year.

The issue here is that BabyMaxPro are thinking of moving their manufacturing business to Lincoln Pharmaceuticals. Given the level of staff unrest, is this still a good idea? Should this be reported to the board? Although this is not urgent, there is a board meeting this morning and you may want to place this on the agenda. It certainly needs more investigation, and you will need to remind everyone of facts; such as how much longer your contract with your current manufacturer will run. You must ensure that the company always has a supplier.

**Item 2:** There has been a break-in at the BabyMaxPro offices. Only one computer has gone missing.

This is a police issue and must be reported immediately. Are you sure that only one computer has gone (sometimes smaller items such as mobile phones or documents are not missed until later)?

The computer is not really the big issue here. What information was on the computer? Was the information backed up? Is this also a company security issue? Why was the building not secure? You will also need to contact your insurance company. (The purchase of a replacement computer could be delegated). This can all be very time consuming.

**Item 3:** You have feedback that your budget figures are incorrect, and there is a board meeting in 20 minutes.

This is urgent and important both for the business and for your career. Calculating figures incorrectly shows a lack of professionalism and attention to detail. This is even worse if large decisions are being made on the back of them! You need to correct these as a matter of urgency, even if it means asking for the item considering budget to be moved down the meeting agenda – perhaps giving you an additional hour.

**Item 4:** Your assistant (a temp) has called in sick with a headache. It is the second time this has happened in two weeks.

Try to delegate this task for now. Ask someone to find you another temp – then later take this up with the agency. If they procrastinate, you need to consider working with another agency. You need to know that you have reliable staff. You also need to consider whether there may be an issue in the workplace. Ink and photocopy fumes can cause headaches – are your rooms well ventilated? You have a duty of care to all staff who work for you, whether they are temporary or permanent.

**Item 5:** You have an email from an angry customer claiming that BabyMaxPro has caused a rash on their child.

This is both important and urgent. In the event of a legal investigation, the way you respond could strengthen or jeopardise your case. Therefore it needs to be handled carefully. You do not want the customer to go to the newspapers saying that you have not responded or have ignored them. For now send a quick holding email, telling the writer that you are very concerned and that you will need to investigate and come back to them. Put this in your diary to do either later that day, or first thing tomorrow.

**Item 6:** John Brown, one of your staff members has announced that he is just about to take his honeymoon! He has been with you for ten years and leaves at midday today. There really ought to be a present for him and his new bride-to-be.

Maintaining staff morale and harmony is hugely important. John has worked at the company a long time. Make a quick calculation (for example £2 per head of general staff, £5 (or more) from more senior staff) and delegate someone to buy a voucher from a main store, to be presented at lunchtime when he leaves. You could even organise an online voucher in two minutes. If you want to ask for the money back from everyone – do that later. The most important thing here is to honour your staff member. Staff goodwill is worth more than a few pounds.

**Item 7:** You have just received an email from a journalist in Australia informing you that toys similar to those in the Learning Range have been seen on sale in Australia under the brand name 'Kismet' – and that the company selling them has Paul Dickinson as director.

This might sound urgent but it could be scaremongering. You need to take your time on this one by first going back to Paul's contract.

Does it specifically say that you have international rights or patent on the toys? What was the agreement? Who are Kismet, and what do they do? How is Paul associated with them? Proof needs to be obtained before you even begin to speak with Paul. It is not an item that should be rushed through in one morning, and you should not be bothering the board until you have all of the facts.

**Item 8:** You have just heard that Stephen Leeming (a guest at the board meeting) has broken down in his car, approximately 15 minutes from the offices.

Could this be delegated? Could someone drive out and collect him? Could this item be moved further down the agenda? Again, this sounds urgent and worrying but actually it is quite fixable and the car can be dealt with later.

**Item 9:** Jan Foreman from Today (a top newspaper) rings to request an interview. She would like the interview to go in the weekend supplement and wants to meet you later today.

Take this seriously, as journalists are known for producing copy whether you agree to be involved or not! Try to find out what the angle is on the story. Could the interview questions be emailed over instead? What about a telephone interview? (Be friendly) would she like any of your stock photos to illustrate the piece? If she insists it must be face-to-face (and you feel it is right to do it) schedule it for later in the day. It will give you time to think and plan – her urgent is not necessarily your urgent.

**Item 10:** Jane Pickles comes in to tell you that money has gone missing from the charity fund jar on her desk. She is very upset.

Could this be linked to the break in? Has anything else gone missing?

Try to calm Jane down and give her something practical to do, such as undertake a quick inventory of the area, informal interviews from others, liaising with the police/insurance. Actions like this are very upsetting for staff. Hold an informal staff meeting later that day and discuss the issue – it could just be a mistake such as someone emptying the jar to store its contents somewhere more safely.

**Item 11:** An inspector from the Health and Safety organisation is waiting in reception. He has decided to do a spot check.

This is important and urgent. Some organisations are allowed to undertake spot checks, and therefore check on the powers of the

Health and Safety Executive. If this is correct, then it is better to allow them to do so by guiding them to a particular part of your business and inviting them to start there. Inform the inspector of the theft issue, and apologise that it is taking up your time, offer them a drink, and allow them to get on with their business. If you try to obstruct or hide anything, you will look suspicious. Most inspectors are either doing an overall check (in which case they just want a quick look at everything and then rush back to type up their report), or in response to a complaint (in which case they will focus on one aspect of your business in great detail). Unless you truly have something to hide, leave them to get on with their check or assign them another member of staff to be their contact, before meeting with them again at the end of their visit.

To help you prepare for in-tray activities, consider the following:

- Think about the job you are applying for, what content are you likely to be given in an in-tray exercise? (Notice that although our two examples are a head teacher and a manager, some of the problems listed are very similar because these types of issues occur in many jobs);

- Remember that activities can be delegated if you have suitable staff (see the organisational chart if there is one);

- Highlight any additional important information such as the date or time;

- Make sure you do exactly what is asked of you, and don't forget to justify your thoughts;

- Use high, medium and low priority groups first, and then prioritise within those;

- Look for any links where two activities can be done at the same time, or conversely remember that the same person cannot be in two places at the same time!

- Never shirk (or delegate) your responsibility.

## Performance Management Exercise

The next exercise that you will need to take, is a Performance Management Exercise. If you've ever taken a role play exercise, then you will be highly familiar with the process of this. If not, fear not, allow us to explain:

The Performance Management Exercise requires you to hold a meeting with a role play actor, who will be playing the part of a character. You will also be playing the part of a character – usually a customer service officer. Prior to the meeting, you will have 20 minutes to read through an information pack, which informs you of the character that you are playing. Following this, you'll go into the room, which will contain the role play actor and an assessor. The actor will be playing the part of someone who has a complaint/or an issue that needs to be discussed. You will need to resolve this issue for them. The exercise will assess you on skills such as:

- Flexibility;

- Communication;

- Leadership;

- Organisation;

- Professionalism.

As before, you will be judged based on how well you can match the core competencies during the meeting. Although you might not necessarily be placed in a police-related scenario during the exercise, the key expectations laid out in your briefing pack will be highly similar to those of an inspector. Therefore, this is an accurate way for the assessors to test your one-to-one interpersonal skills.

Now, let's look at how to handle one of these scenarios. For the purposes of this example, we'll assume that you are acting in the role of customer services officer. Please note that there is no guarantee you'll be asked to play this role. However, this is a very commonly used trope in role play exercises, so it's a good idea to prepare for this.

## Preparation Phase

Although the preparation phase is not assessable, you must still use the time wisely.

This is how we recommend you use the time:

- Quickly read the scenario and any supporting information/ documentation. If you have already studied the Welcome Pack prior to assessment, your life will be a lot easier.

- Once you have studied the scenario and any additional information/ documentation, you should then separate relevant information from irrelevant information. Write down brief notes as to what you think is relevant.

- You now need to cross match any relevant information from the scenario with procedures, policies and your responsibilities that are provided in the Welcome Pack. For example, if within the scenario it becomes apparent that somebody from the centre is being bullied or harassed, you will need to know, use and make reference to the equality policy statement during the activity phase of the assessment. Another example would be where a child has been reported missing. If this was the case, then you would possibly wish to make use of the security guards, the tannoy system and also the CCTV cameras that are based around the centre.

We would now recommend that you write down on your note paper a step by step approach as what you intend to do during the activity stage. An example of this may be as follows:

## STEP 1

Introduce yourself to the role actor and ask him/her how you can help them.

(Remember to be polite and respectful and treat the role play actor in a sensitive and supportive manner. You are being assessed against the core competency of respect for race and diversity during every role play scenario)

## STEP 2

Listen to them carefully and ask relevant questions to establish the facts.

(How, When, Where, Why, Who)

## STEP 3

Clarify the information received, to check you have understood exactly what has happened.

## STEP 4

Provide a suitable solution to the problem or situation, and tell the role play actor what you intend to do.

(Remember to use keywords and phrases from the core competencies)

## STEP 5

Check to confirm that the role play actor is happy with your solution. Provide a final summary of what you intend to do, and ask them if there is anything else you can help them.

(Tell the role actor that you will take responsibility for solving the problem and that you will keep them updated on progress)

Once you have made your notes and created a plan of action you are now ready to go through to the activity phase. Before we move on to this stage of the role play assessment we will provide you with a further explanation of how you may wish to approach the preparation phase, using a sample scenario.

### Sample Performance Management Exercise 1

You are the customer service manager at a fictitious retail centre. A member of your staff approaches you and tells you that she has been bullied by another member of staff. The woman is clearly upset by the situation and she wants you to take action.

### How to Prepare

If you have already taken the time to study the Welcome Pack prior to attending the assessment, then the first thing that will spring to your mind will be the equality policy statement.

Within the statement you will find specific details about how to deal with situations of this nature and it is essential that you follow each step carefully. Remember that one of the assessable core competencies requires you to gather all relevant information (decision making).

Using my 5 step plan, the following is how you might deal with this type of situation:

**STEP 1** – Walk into the activity room and introduce yourself to the role actor. Ask them sensitively what the problem was and how you can help them. If there is a chair available in the room, then ask them to sit down.

**STEP 2** – Listen very carefully to what they have to say, and sympathise where appropriate. You can then start to establish the facts of the case, asking them relevant questions such as:

- How long had the bullying been going on for?

- Who was involved and what had they been doing/ saying?

- Were any other people involved?

- Have there been any witnesses to this incident?

- Had they asked the other person to stop bullying them and if so what was their reaction?

**STEP 3** – You should then clarify and confirm with the role actor that you have gathered the correct facts.

**STEP 4** – At this stage, take full control of the situation and tell the role actor what you intend to do about the situation. Make reference to the equality policy statement, and use it as a basis for solving the problem. You should also use keywords and phrases that match the core competencies.

**STEP 5** – During the final stages of the role play activity stage, check to confirm that the role play actor is happy with your solution. Provide them with a final summary of what you intend to do, and ask them if there is anything else that you can help them with. At this stage, you should also confirm that you are going to take responsibility for resolving the problem, and that you will keep them updated on progress as and when it occurs.

### The Activity Phase

The activity stage will again last for 5 minutes and it is during this phase that you are required to interact with the role actor.

During the activity stage there will be an assessor in the room whose responsibility it is to assess you against the core competencies. Try to ignore them and concentrate fully on how you interact with the role actor. There may also be a third person in the room who will be there to shadow the assessor or for quality assurance purposes. During the activity stage you will be assessed on what you did and how you did it.

During the previous sample role play exercise (exercise 1) we focused on a complaint made by a member of staff who claimed that she was being bullied by another member of staff.

Within the equality policy statement you will find suggested courses of action. The options here may suggest that the person asks the offender to stop, the problem is discussed with an appropriate person (you) or the option is available to make a formal complaint.

Below we have provided you with some suggested responses to this type of exercise followed by an explanation. Most of these can be applied to similar exercises surrounding harassment cases, although you should judge every situation separately and act according to the brief.

### SAMPLE RESPONSES AND ACTIONS TO EXERCISE 1

*"Thank you for coming to see me today. I understand that you have a problem with another member of staff?"*

During this type of response, you are demonstrating a level of customer care and you are focusing on the needs of the individual. Remember to use open body language and never become confrontational, defensive or aggressive.

*"Would you be able to tell me exactly what has happened and how this has affected you? I will also need to ask you who has been bullying you, where it has been occurring and on how many occasions including dates and times."*

Again you are focusing on the needs of the individual, which is important. Try to look and sound genuine and also use suitable facial expressions. In order to 'problem solve' you must first ask questions and gather the facts of the incident.

*"It must be very difficult for you to bring this matter to my attention; you are to be praised for this course of action."*

During this response, you are demonstrating a caring nature and you are providing a high level of service.

*"Have you asked him to stop or have you informed anybody else of this situation?"*

and

*"Are you aware of this happening to anybody else?"*

Here you are gathering the facts, which will help you provide a suitable resolution to the problem.

*"The company equality policy in relation to this kind of alleged behaviour is quite clear, it states XYZ. It will NOT be tolerated and I can assure you the matter will be dealt with."*

During this response, you are detailing the company equality policy. This demonstrates to the assessor that you are fully aware of the policies and procedures – this will gain you higher scores. You are also stating that this type of behaviour is not accepted and you are, therefore, challenging the inappropriate behaviour in line with the police inspector core competencies.

*"Before I detail my solution to this problem I want to first of all confirm the details of the case. Please can you confirm that...."*

During this response, I am confirming and checking that the details I have obtained are correct.

*"Please be aware that you can make a formal complaint if you so wish? Your feelings and wishes are paramount during my investigation. What would you like to happen from here? Would you like to make a formal complaint against the individual concerned?"*

By asking the complainant what they want to do, you are demonstrating that you are putting their needs first and you are respecting confidentiality.

*"Let me assure you that this matter will be dealt with as a priority but in the meantime I will place another member of staff with you so that*

*you can work in a comfortable environment. Are you happy with this course of action?"*

Here you are taking action to resolve the problem. You are also informing the person how you intend to resolve it. Finally you are checking that the person is happy with your actions.

*"May I thank you again for bringing this matter to my attention; I will keep you fully informed of all progress. I wish to inform you that I will be taking personal responsibility for resolving this issue. Is there anything else I can do for you?"*

Finally you are demonstrating a high level of service and also checking if there is anything else that you can do for them. You are also taking personal responsibility for resolving the issue. It is important to tell them that you will keep them informed of the outcome of any investigation.

## TOP TIPS FOR PREPARING FOR THE PERFORMANCE MANAGEMENT EXERCISES

- Learn the core competencies that are being assessed and be able to 'act' out each one;

- A good way to practice for these exercises is to get a friend or family relative to 'role play' the sample exercises contained within this guide;

- When practicing the exercises, try to pick someone you know who will make it difficult for you. Also, try to resolve each issue in a calm but effective manner, in line with the core competencies.

## TOP TIPS FOR PASSING FOR THE PERFORMANCE MANAGEMENT EXERCISES

- Use the preparation time wisely;

- Learn the pre-assessment material before you go to the assessment. This will make your life much easier;

- Remain calm during every role play. Even if the actor becomes confrontational, it is essential that you remain calm and in control;

- If at any time during the role play activity phase the actor uses language that is either inappropriate (including swearing), discriminatory or uses any form of harassment then you must challenge it immediately;

- When challenging this kind of behaviour you must do so in an assertive manner without becoming aggressive. Always be polite and respectful at all times;

- Use effective listening skills during the role play exercises and ask questions in order to gather the facts;

- Once you have gathered the facts of the case or situation then solve the problem.

On the following page, we have provided you with a sample Performance Management exercise. Read the exercise carefully and then take notes in the box, providing details of how you might deal with the situation. Make sure you have a copy of the core competencies to hand when making your notes.

Next, get a friend or relative to act out the scenario, so you can practise dealing with it.

## Sample Performance Management Exercise 2

You are the customer services officer at a fictitious retail centre. A school teacher has lost a pupil in the shopping centre and he wants to discuss the matter with you. He is very annoyed that it took him so long to find your office. He states that there were no security staff around and his pupil has now been missing for fifteen minutes.

He wants to know what you intend to do about it.

## How to prepare and possible actions:

- Are there any security staff that could help look for any missing persons?;

- Is there a police station within the complex and can the police be used to respond to situations like this?;

- Request the attendance of the police immediately;

- Make sure that you keep the teacher in the office with you so that they can provide further information to the police about the missing child;

- Try to gather information about the missing child – How old are they? What are they wearing? What is their name?  Where were they last seen?;

- Try to reassure the teacher that everything will be ok;

- If there is the option of using a loudspeaker system in the shopping centre, then this could be used to transmit a 'missing persons' message;

- Consider the option of using the centre's CCTV cameras to locate the missing person;

- Consider positioning a member of the security team at each exit to prevent anybody walking out with the child.

On the following page, we have provided a sample response to this exercise. Read it before using the box on the following page to take notes on how you would deal with this situation:

## Sample responses and actions to exercise 2

*"Hello sir, my name is Richard and I'm the customer service officer for this centre. I understand that one of your pupils has gone missing in the centre – is that correct?" (Establish exactly what has happened)."*

*"Firstly can I reassure you that the police have been called and they are on their way. I have also put a security guard at each exit to look out for the missing child. In the meantime, I would like to take some notes from you."*

*"Please can you give me a full description of the missing pupil please including their name?" (Make a list of the description.)"*

*"Please can you tell me how long ago they have been missing for and where they were last seen?"*

*"Have you or anybody else been looking for the missing person and have you reported this to anybody else yet?"*

*"Is there a possibility that they might have wandered off to their favourite shop or gone somewhere else with another parent who was in the group?"*

*"Do you think they would understand their own name if we broadcast this over the loudspeaker system?"*

*"OK Sir, thank you for providing me with these details. This is what I propose to do in order to resolve the situation. To begin with I will check the CCTV cameras to see if we can locate the missing child. I will also put out a tannoy announcement asking the missing child to go to the nearest customer services desk where a member of staff will meet them."*

*"In addition to this course of action I will also put the registered nurse on standby so that she can treat the child for shock if appropriate."*

*"In the meantime please stay here until the police arrive, as it is important you provide them with more information. Let me reassure you that we will do everything we possibly can to locate the missing person. I will be taking personal responsibility for resolving this issue and I will keep you updated on progress as and when it occurs."*

## Notes for sample performance management exercise 2

| Presentation |
| --- |

Do presentations make you feel nervous? If you have that sinking feeling, then don't despair. For assessment centre presentations, you need to feel sufficiently anxious to create immediacy and a little frisson, but not so nervous that you become debilitated by the process.

There are two aspects we need to look at here:

1. Your material.

2. You!

## Your material

Let's start with your material. Once you have your material in order and organised, then you will find that you are more than halfway there. Being organised and knowing the points you want to get across, will give you confidence, which will go a long way to helping you when you are facing your assessors.

First of all, it helps to be familiar with the situation. You will probably be asked to present to a group of around 2-6 people, who will most probably be sitting in front of you.

You do not have to stand, but it can look too casual if you sit (and of course there may not be a chair set out for you) – in which case, plan on standing, and then if you are invited to sit, you can.

## How to Pass

You should be told in advance the equipment that will be at your disposal. If you are not given this information, try to contact police personnel beforehand to check. It could throw you completely if you turn up with a set of slides, only to find there is no equipment in the room.

There is no problem with simply standing and delivering your presentation, with heart, and no materials or technology at all. The important point is that you feel comfortable, and that your presentation represents you. For example, if you were presenting to motivate sales professionals, a set of cold slides would achieve less than a more personal rousing motivational call to action.

To conclude, use the materials that suit both your style and the subject matter. For example, if you want to convey a complex notion or figure comparison, it helps to have that pictorially as a diagram or chart. However, if the job involved sales, you may not need slides at all, and prefer to use your personal charm and personality to get your message across.

Important point: – think about what you are attempting to convey. How complex is the material? How much do you want them to see your personality shining through? How important is it that you are personally convincing?

Finally you will be told when to start, and you should have been given a guide as to how long you are expected to speak for. Between five and twenty minutes is usual. This gives you long enough to structure a presentation and represent yourself, but not so long that the panel are there all day.

The assessment panel will be timing you, and therefore it is ESSENTIAL that you are able to keep to that time. Presentations are a key part of management and the ability to keep to time is a skill that demonstrates personal control. Overrun and you may have points deducted from your performance, and you cannot afford to make silly mistakes like that.

### Structuring material

Even if you are not going to produce slides, it helps to think in terms of slides (or cue cards) as they are easy to remember and give you structure.

Whether you then use them or not will depend on you and your delivery style.

Having a clear structure is hugely important. It will:

- Enable you to provide a cohesive argument;
- Enable your audience or panel to follow through your points;
- Provide you with an easy 'roadmap' to follow, should you drift off course or lose confidence.

Your presentation needs to be balanced and even in content, and therefore it helps to separate it out into chunks. A rule of thumb is that each slide should carry only basic information and allow for 2-3 minutes of speaking time, at which point the presenter can discuss the points made on the slide.

In addition, there will be an introduction slide and an end slide. Let's illustrate this as an example. Imagine you have been asked to produce a 15-minute presentation on 'Green issues in the office environment.'

This information helps us to calculate that for a 15-minute presentation we need:

- One introductory slide that has a title or heading and our name;

- No more than 5 slides for the main part of our talk (at just under 3-minute search);

- One final slide that either says 'Any questions?' or 'Thank you'.

Now that you know you only have five slides to get your point across in main section of the presentation, you will need to make each slide work hard within a structure or argument. Therefore, we could pull together:

An introductory slide – the title of your presentation, together with your name.

Slide 1 – why offices need to consider green issues with a list of points.

Slide 2 – where considering green issues can have an impact on the environment and business.

Slide 3 – a list of easy ways that can incorporate green issues into office life, for example, recycling

Slide 4 – a list of benefits to staff and the business

Slide 5 – what you intend to (or the business could) do about it – actions

Final slide – summary and a call for any questions.

Important point – do not cram information onto your slide or paper. Try to have no more than five bullet points on each slide, under the heading, and if you need to show something complex such as a spreadsheet, build in time allocation for your audience to read it. By doing this, you have delivered exactly what they asked for and have not overrun, in a neat little presentation that has structure, but has also allowed you to present your views and demonstrate your personality – perfect!

Now have a go at this yourself, using the method above. Imagine that you have been asked you to come up with a very general 15 minute presentation on 'The future for staff development in your organisation.' Have a go at structuring some slides with just your initial thoughts below.

**Introductory slide:**

_(blank box)_

**Slide 1**

_(blank box)_

**Slide 2**

**Slide 3**

**Slide 4**

**Slide 5**

**Summary slide**

How did you get on? You could have put anything, as there is no right answer, but here is an example of how you could have done it:

**Introductory slide:**

The future for staff development in our organisation my name

**Slide 1**

Perhaps a quote about learning or a definition of what development means

**Slide 2**

Some points regarding what we do to develop staff at the moment (and maybe some statistics?)

**Slide 3**

What is the trend in the 'wider world' at the present time?

**Slide 4**

The benefits of incorporating some of the ideas of others.

**Slide 5**

What this actually means we have to do – action points.

**Summary slide**

Thank you

Any questions?

Remember that philosophising is all very well, but some good strong action points will serve you well and may get you more marks. (Note that if you don't include HOW you are going to do something, consider it anyway as you may be asked at the end of your presentation). It is too easy to say, 'We must change the culture' without saying actually how you intend to achieve that, and you would not want to be put on the spot without an answer.

**Quick tip**: Most of the presentation topics or questions that you will be asked to present will be a) asking you to look into the future, and b) what you would do? For example: If you were the manager of the new team, what would be your strategy and your first priority actions? Or 'If you were fortunate to secure the job, what changes would you make to the culture and how?

**You**

Remember that the image and mood you want to convey is that of professional competence. This does not mean that you cannot deliver a light-hearted speech but it must be appropriate to the situation and be natural – therefore no contrived jokes!

You should now be clear about your material, and that should give you some confidence. Draw yourself up to your full height, and ensure that your head is looking forward and nicely balanced, not up at the sky or down at your feet.

If you are presenting from a standing position, stand with your feet slightly apart, to give you a good solid base. Keep your hands at your sides or clasped in front of you. Your job is to 'put some flesh on those bones' with your description of the key words. Talk around the bullet points, but engage and speak with your audience – again not at the screen (if there is one).

**Nerves**

Whilst some nerves are totally understandable and acceptable, but what can you do to stop them running away altogether?

Remember to keep breathing! This may sound odd, but when we get nervous we take in less oxygen and breathe at a faster and more shallow rate. This does not deliver sufficient oxygen to where it is needed and we begin to feel light headed and anxious. Our main reaction is to try to access more oxygen by breathing faster, but actually what we should be doing is taking in deeper breaths. Therefore, slow your breathing down and take deeper, more meaningful breaths (this will also slow your speech down, which is helpful as we tend to speak faster when we are tense).

If you have the tendency to shake, then stand firm. Imagine that you are a tree with roots that go down into the ground and feel rooted to the spot. Sit down if you prefer, and try to resist bringing attention to your nervousness, as it is very possible that no one has noticed.

**Eye contact**

It is as simple as this – look at your audience and speak TO them, not AT them. In a business setting, these people will be your future team and you will have a good rapport with them – remember it is only for today that it may feel awkward.

Smile and look directly at everyone. Speak in the same way that you would if you were speaking to your family or colleagues. Engaging everyone is important, and that is something you can do by simply looking into their eyes.

**Personality**

Try to be yourself. This might sound corny, but each of us has a presenting style that is natural to us. Unless you have had feedback in the past that you need to change your style – accept how you present and see it as an extension of your style.

Remember that the panel do not want to see a load of clones. There is something satisfying in noting that someone has a unique style that defines them, and that they can use that style to reach out to the audience.

Just to recap:

1. Be prepared with all your notes in order.

2. Take deep breaths (without gasping) to lower your anxiety.

3. Smile and make good eye contact with your assessors before starting. This will set a good tone for your presentation.

4. Do not try to stifle your natural style.

5. If you are standing, make sure you have a solid base.

6. Keep any important notes to hand and one eye on the clock.

7. Present with confidence, knowing that your material is good and that you have prepared well.

## Cognitive Ability Tests

The final written based assessment, is a series of cognitive ability tests. These will consist of:

• A verbal reasoning test;

• A numerical reasoning test;

• An inductive reasoning test.

These tests will be taken under exam conditions, and you'll complete the tests along with a number of other candidates, in a large assessment room. Prior to each test, you will be given the chance to take a practice version, so that you have some idea of what to expect.

The cognitive ability tests are the only area of the assessment centre where you won't be tested based on the competency areas. You will be graded based on your score in each test, and will then be given a mark based on all your overall performance across all of the tests.

Although you will be given a chance to take a practice test, this doesn't mean that you should rest on your laurels. These tests are possibly the most difficult part of the assessment centre to pass, and therefore it's essential that you conduct thorough preparation well before you attend. To help you do this, we've provided you with information on what to expect from each test, and some practice questions!

## Verbal Reasoning

Verbal Reasoning tests are specifically designed to assess a candidate's ability to reason with words, language or comprehension, and demonstrate a solid understanding of written information within the English language.

The ability to spell words correctly, use correct grammar and punctuation, understand word meanings and interpret written information, is an imperative skill that is required in a range of situations and job roles. Thus, it is important that you are able to demonstrate these skills to a high standard and perform to the best of your ability. As a police inspector, you will be filling in large amounts of paper work, sending emails and letters, and generally maintaining frequent levels of communication with other agencies and within your own constabulary. For this reason, it's vital that you can demonstrate a reasonable level of spelling, grammar and punctuation.

### What does a verbal test consist of?

Verbal Reasoning tests can and do come in different formats. Be sure to find out what type of test it is you are going to be sitting. This will help you to practice the questions to the best of your ability. Even if you are required to sit a particular test i.e. a Verbal Comprehension test, it is best to practice a range of verbal tests to ensure that you are ready for anything that might be used in your actual assessment.

Typical formats of the verbal test include:

- Verbal Logical Reasoning;

- Verbal Reasoning;

- Verbal Comprehension;

- Vocabulary test;

- Spelling and Grammar test;

- Word Meanings test;

- Word Relations test.

The most common type of verbal ability test, is a reading and comprehension exercise. The purpose of a reading and comprehension exercise, is to test your attention to detail. In each question, you'll be given a passage, and then asked to answer questions based on the passage. Below we've included a sample question, to give you some idea of how to go about completing this:

## Animal euthanasia

Animal euthanasia is the practice of terminating the life of an animal in a painless or minimally painful way in order to stop suffering or other undesired conditions in life.

This may be voluntary or involuntary, and carried out with or without a physician. In a medical environment, this can be carried out by oral, intravenous or intramuscular drug administration. Laws around the world vary greatly with regard to animal euthanasia and are constantly subject to change as cultural values shift and better palliative care or treatments become available. Reasons for animal euthanasia include:

- Terminal illness – e.g. cancer;
- Rabies;
- Behavioural problems (that usually cannot be corrected) – e.g. aggression;
- Illness or broken limbs that would cause suffering for the animal to live with, or when the owner cannot afford (or has a moral objection to) treatment;
- Old age – Deterioration to loss of major bodily functions. Severe impairment of the quality of life;
- Lack of homes – Some shelters receive considerably more surrendered animals than they are capable of re-housing. This may be attributed to irresponsible owners who do not spay or neuter pets, causing unwanted litters. Some pets turned in to animal shelters are not adopted out.

**A** = TRUE    **B** = FALSE  **C** = IMPOSSIBLE TO SAY

### Question 1

Shifts in cultural values are the main causes for changes in the law around the world in relation to animal euthanasia.

### Question 2

Animal testing is cruel and immoral.

## Question 3

Irresponsible owners who do not spay or neuter pets may be the cause of some shelters receiving more surrendered animals than they are capable of re-housing.

## How To Answer This Question

Q1. The answer to this question is C, IMPOSSIBLE TO SAY. The reason for this is that while the passage states that shifts in cultural values have an impact upon animal euthanasia laws, it doesn't specify this as being the main reason.

Q2. The answer to this question is C, IMPOSSIBLE TO SAY. The passage does not mention the impact on animal testing. Only answer using information from the passage, and do not let your personal feelings change your answer.

Q3. The answer to this question is A, TRUE. The passage clearly states that this is the case.

Now that you've looked at how to answer one of these, have a go at the following questions:

## VERBAL ABILITY – READING AND COMPREHENSION

For this section, you need to read the passage carefully and answer the questions that follow. For each question/statement, you need to determine whether it is true, false or impossible to say.

*An accident occurred on the M6 motorway between junctions 8 and 9 southbound at 3pm. The driver of a Ford Fiesta was seen to pull into the middle lane without indicating, forcing another car to veer into the central reservation. One person suffered a broken arm and was taken to hospital before the police arrived.*

**A = TRUE   B = FALSE   C = IMPOSSIBLE TO SAY**

### Question 1

The accident was on the M6 motorway on the carriageway that leads to Scotland.

### Question 2

The driver of the ford Fiesta was injured in the crash.

### Question 3

The central reservation was responsible for the accident.

### Question 4

The police did not give first aid at the scene.

### Question 5

The accident happened at 1500 hours.

*Following a bank robbery in a town centre, 6 masked gunmen were seen speeding away from the scene in a black van. The incident, which happened in broad daylight in front of hundreds of shoppers, was picked up by CCTV footage. Police are appealing for witnesses. The local newspaper has offered a £5,000 reward for any information leading to the arrest of all the people involved.*

**A =** TRUE    **B =** FALSE    **C =** IMPOSSIBLE TO SAY

### Question 6

The vehicle in which the gunmen drove off was a black van.

### Question 7

Someone must have seen something.

### Question 8

The incident was picked up by CCTV cameras.

### Question 9

The newspaper will pay £5,000 for information leading to the arrest of all the men involved.

### Question 10

Police are not appealing to members of the public for help.

*At 1800 hours today, police issued a statement in relation to the crime scene on Armstrong Road. Police have been examining the scene all day and reports suggest that it may be murder. Forensic officers have been visiting the incident and inform us that the whole street has been cornered off and nobody will be allowed through. Police say that the street involved will be closed for another 18 hours and no access will be available to anyone during this time.*

**A = TRUE   B = FALSE   C = IMPOSSIBLE TO SAY**

### Question 11

Police have confirmed the incident is murder.

### Question 12

Forensic officers have now left the scene.

### Question 13

The road will be open at 12 noon the following day.

### Question 14

Although the street has been cornered off, taxis and buses will be given access.

### Question 15

Forensic officers will be at the scene all night.

*During the summer Mrs Olds called Neslington Country Council on 12 occasions reporting anti-social behaviour. Twenty-five-per-cent of the calls were about local drunk Andy Young loitering and discarding empty beer cans in her garden. Half of all the calls were because local teenagers were causing a nuisance around her semi-detached house, including disturbing behaviour and criminal damage. Mrs Olds reported that she felt scared in her own home.*

*The only facts known at this stage are:*

- *Local teenagers have been stopped by police and found with alcohol near Mrs Olds property;*

- *Two calls were because next door neighbours were playing music too loud;*

- *The Ford family live next door to Mr and Mrs Olds;*

- *Mrs Old's husband is retired;*

- *Mrs Olds lives next to a park where teenagers are frequent;*

- *A neighbour, Mr Cook, has been warned about playing music too loud.*

**A = TRUE    B = FALSE    C = IMPOSSIBLE TO SAY**

## Question 16

Mrs Olds called the council three times about Andy Young.

## Question 17

Mrs Olds is retired.

## Question 18

Mrs Olds reported Mr Cook twice for playing his music too loud.

## Question 19

The park is possibly a reason the anti-social behaviour occurs.

## Question 20

Alcohol is the main cause of the anti-social behaviour.

This morning at 6am, Shepham Police raided a property with a warrant to search it for drugs. They found a selection of items commonly used to grow cannabis and a number of small cannabis plants. Police are still searching the property.

The latest reported facts are:

- The house is owned by Amanda Holder;

- She lives in the property with her partner, Michael Smith and his son, James Smith;

- Amanda and James do not get along;

- Michael works on an oil rig and has been away from home for two months;

- The drug growing equipment was found in James' room;

- All three have previous convictions for possessing drugs.

**A** = TRUE   **B** = FALSE   **C** = IMPOSSIBLE TO SAY

### Question 21

Amanda Holder has been convicted of producing drugs before.

### Question 22

The door of the house was damaged in the drug raid.

### Question 23

Michael may not be aware of the drugs.

### Question 24

James may have been growing the drugs to spite Amanda.

### Question 25

Michael may have planted the cannabis plants a month ago.

*A young child disappeared from a local food shop in Kinston after her mother became distracted at the counter. The mother asked the shop assistant to ring Kinston Police when she discovered her child had disappeared. The police arrived 10-minutes after they were called. Another shopper reported the child being walked away from the shop by a male who was approximately 6ft tall, with brown hair.*

*The only facts known at this stage are:*

- *The mother Miss Jenkins has red hair;*

- *Police were called at 10:25am on Saturday morning;*

- *Miss Jenkins had spoken to her child's father 10-minutes prior to her disappearance;*

- *The child's name is Molly;*

- *Molly's father has brown hair and is approximately 5ft 11;*

- *Tony Woods has a child with Miss Jenkins.*

**A = TRUE   B = FALSE   C = IMPOSSIBLE TO SAY**

## Question 26

The police arrived at the scene at 10:25am Saturday morning.

## Question 27

Tony Woods is Molly's father.

## Question 28

Molly's father may have taken her.

## Question 29

Molly disappeared from a food shop in Kinston.

## Question 30

Molly must have red or brown hair.

*ANSWERS TO VERBAL ABILITY*
*READING AND COMPREHENSION*

**Q1. C = Impossible to say**

**Q2. C = Impossible to say**

**Q3. B = False**

**Q4. C = Impossible to say**

**Q5. A = True**

**Q6. A = True**

**Q7. C = Impossible to say**

**Q8. A = True**

**Q9. A = True**

**Q10. B = False**

**Q11. B = False**

**Q12. C = Impossible to say**

**Q13. A = True**

**Q14. B = False**

**Q15. C = Impossible to say**

**Q16. A = True**

**Q17. C = Impossible to say**

**Q18. C = Impossible to say**

**Q19. A = True**

**Q20. C = Impossible to say**

**Q21. C = Impossible to say**

**Q22. C = Impossible to say**

**Q23. A = True**

**Q24. A = True**

**Q25. B = False**

**Q26. B = False**

**Q27. C = Impossible to say**

**Q28. A = True**

**Q29. A = True**

**Q30. B = False**

## Numerical Reasoning

The second type of test that you will need to take, is a numerical reasoning assessment. This test measures your ability to solve mathematical problems and equations.

## WHAT ARE NUMERICAL REASONING TESTS?

A Numerical Reasoning test is designed to assess mathematical knowledge through number-related assessments. Numerical Reasoning is one of the most common forms of psychometric testing, and enables employers to filter out strong candidates from those less desirable. Most recruitment processes now contain a form of psychometric and aptitude testing; so it is important that you are 100% prepared!

Numerical Reasoning tests cover a wide range of mathematical formulas; and so it is imperative to comprehend the skills and knowledge required to work out the mathematics involved. Most Numerical Reasoning tests contain questions in relation to:

| Adding | Subtracting | Dividing | Multiplying |
|---|---|---|---|
| Fractions | Percentages | Decimals | Ratios |
| Charts and Graphs | Mean, Mode, Median, Range | Areas and Perimeters | Number Sequences |
| Time | Conversions | Measurements | Money |
| Proportions | Formulae | Data Interpretation | Quantitative Data |
| Data Analysis | Correlations | Statistics | Shapes |

## WHAT SKILLS ARE MEASURED?

Obviously, a Numerical Reasoning test primarily deals with assessing your level of mathematical ability. Other skills that are also measured, and often assessed by examiners are:

- Critical Reasoning;

- General Knowledge and Intelligence;

- Estimations;

- Speed;

- Concentration;

- Analysis;

- Interpretation.

## PREPARING FOR A NUMERICAL REASONING TEST

Your performance in a Numerical Reasoning test can undoubtedly be bettered through practice! Getting to grips with the format of the test, and gaining an insight of the typical questions you are likely to face can only work to your advantage.

The more you practice, the more you will see your performance excel! With any psychometric testing, it is important to fully maximise your skills and knowledge prior to your assessment to ensure the best result.

This comprehensive guide will provide you with lots of sample questions, similar to those that will be found on your Numerical Reasoning test. Our insightful and ultimate preparation guide will allow you to grasp each question type, understand what is expected, and show you how to achieve the correct answer.

## WHAT TYPES OF NUMERICAL TESTS ARE THERE?

As previously mentioned, Numerical Reasoning tests vary in their format in terms of questions and level of difficulty; but foremost, they all test similar arithmetic. Numerical Reasoning tests are often classified through two means: Formats and Level of Difficulty.

Numerical reasoning is essential for a police inspector. A large part of your job will involve dealing with numbers and figures; whether you are assessing crime rate figures or working out budgets for the constabulary, you can expect to be using your mathematical skills on a regular basis.

In order for you to gain the best knowledge and practice, the following testing section will include a variety of question types, to ensure you are fully prepared for any Numerical Reasoning test that you may be required to sit.

The most common type of Numerical Reasoning test that you will have to face at the assessment centre, is a data interpretation test. This is a test that will examine your ability to deal with large amounts of numbers and statistics. Take a look below for an example:

*Based on 100 students. Marks in English Maths and Science Examinations.*

| MARKS OUT OF 40 | | | | |
|---|---|---|---|---|
| Subject | 30 or above | 20 or above | 10 or above | 0 or above |
| English | 19 | 52 | 91 | 100 |
| Maths | 13 | 36 | 90 | 100 |
| Science | 11 | 42 | 87 | 100 |
| | | | | |
| Average | 11 | 43 | 89 | 100 |

## Question 1

If at least 50% in their examination is needed to go on to higher education, how many students in Maths can go on to higher education?

| A | B | C | D | E |
|---|---|---|---|---|
| 49 | 13 | 36 | 19 | 27 |

## Question 2

What is the percentage of students who achieved marks of 20 or above in their English exam?

| A | B | C | D | E |
|---|---|---|---|---|
| 36% | 41% | 56% | 52% | 48% |

## Question 3

What is the difference between the number of students who achieved 30 or above in English, and the number of students who achieved 20 or above in Science?

| A | B | C | D | E |
|---|---|---|---|---|
| 23 | 25 | 27 | 31 | 19 |

## Question 4

Using the box labelled 'average', work out the number of students who scored less than 50%.

| A | B | C | D | E |
|---|---|---|---|---|
| 43 | 57 | 21 | 17 | 53 |

## Question 5

What subject had the highest number of students who scored below 10?

| A | B | C | D | E |
|---|---|---|---|---|
| English | Maths | Science | All the same | English and Maths |

# How To Answer

Q1. C = 36

EXPLANATION = 50% of 40 = 20. Number of students who scored 20 and above in Maths = 36.

Q2. D = 52%

EXPLANATION = 100 students, 52 students achieved marks of 20 or above = 52%.

Q3. A = 23

EXPLANATION = Number of students with 30 or above in English = 19. Students with 20 or above in Science = 42. So 42 -19 = 23.

Q4. B = 57

EXPLANATION = 50% of 40 = 20. Number of students who scored 20 marks or above for average = 43. So, 100 – 43 = 57.

Q5. C = Science

EXPLANATION = scores of 10 or below = English = 9, Maths = 10, Science = 13

## Practice Test

Study the following chart and answer the four questions that follow.

*Bike Sales*

| Country | Jan | Feb | Mar | April | May | June | Total |
|---------|-----|-----|-----|-------|-----|------|-------|
| UK | 21 | 28 | 15 | 35 | 31 | 20 | 150 |
| Germany | 45 | 48 | 52 | 36 | 41 | 40 | 262 |
| France | 32 | 36 | 33 | 28 | 20 | 31 | 180 |
| Brazil | 42 | 41 | 37 | 32 | 35 | 28 | 215 |
| Spain | 22 | 26 | 17 | 30 | 24 | 22 | 141 |
| Italy | 33 | 35 | 38 | 28 | 29 | 38 | 201 |
| Total | 195 | 214 | 192 | 189 | 180 | 179 | 1149 |

## Question 1

What percentage of the overall total was sold in April?

| A | B | C | D | E |
|---|---|---|---|---|
| 17.8% | 17.2% | 18.9% | 16.4% | 21.6% |

## Question 2

What percentage of the overall total sales were bikes' sold to the French importer? To one decimal place.

| A | B | C | D | E |
|---|---|---|---|---|
| 15.7% | 18.2% | 18.9% | 25.6% | 24.5% |

## Question 3

What is the average number of units per month imported to Brazil over the first 4 months of the year?

| A | B | C | D | E |
|---|---|---|---|---|
| 28 | 24 | 32 | 38 | 40 |

## Question 4

What month saw the biggest increase in total sales from the previous month?

| A | B | C | D | E |
|---|---|---|---|---|
| January | February | March | April | May |

Study the following chart and answer the four questions that follow.

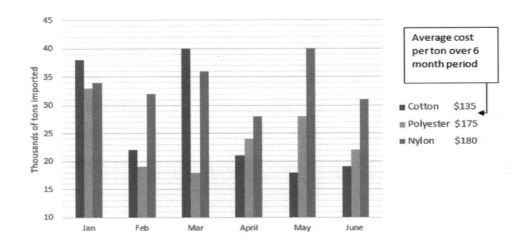

## Question 5

What was the mean value for nylon imported over the 6 month period?

| A | B | C | D | E |
|---|---|---|---|---|
| 42.5 | 18.5 | 33.5 | 49.5 | 37.5 |

## Question 6

What was the range for polyester imports across the 6 month period?

| A | B | C | D | E |
|---|---|---|---|---|
| 15 | 21 | 23 | 52 | 51 |

## Question 7

What was the difference between cotton material and nylon material imports in the first 3 months of the year?

| A | B | C | D | E |
|---|---|---|---|---|
| 5 | 15 | 24 | 17 | 2 |

## Question 8

What was the approximate ratio of polyester and nylon material imports in the first 4 months of the year?

| A | B | C | D | E |
|---|---|---|---|---|
| 94: 120 | 94: 130 | 92: 110 | 95: 100 | 94:90 |

## Question 9

There are 60 girls and 65 boys in the lunch hall at school. What is the ratio of girls to boys? Give your answer in its simplest form.

Answer [          ]

## Question 10

Look carefully for the pattern, and then choose which pair of numbers comes next.

1,   3,   6,   10,   15,   21,   28

| A | B | C | D | E |
|---|---|---|---|---|
| 42, 56 | 42, 48 | 30, 36 | 32, 36 | 36, 45 |

## Question 11

The lowest percentage for attendance in Year 7 was 51%. The highest attendance was 100%. The median percent for attendance is 70%. The lower quartile percent was 61% and the upper quartile percent was 90%. Represent this information with a box-and-whisker plot.

## Question 12

What is the amount of the lower quartile?

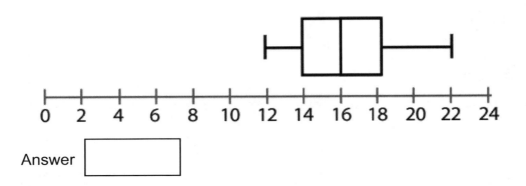

Answer [　　　　　]

## Question 13

The set of data below shows the results in a year 11 Media mock exam. The marks are out of 100%. The teacher wants to find the mean mark for this test, which was given to 68 pupils. Give your answer to 1 decimal place.

The mean mark is: 

| Media mock exam (%) | No. of pupils | No. of pupils X media mock exam (%) |
|:---:|:---:|:---:|
| 10 | 0 | 10 X 0 = 0 |
| 20 | 2 | 20 X 2 = 40 |
| 30 | 3 | |
| 40 | 6 | |
| 50 | 8 | |
| 60 | 11 | |
| 70 | 8 | |
| 80 | 15 | |
| 90 | 12 | |
| 100 | 3 | |
| Totals | 68 | |

## Question 14

The two way table shown compares pupils' results for GCSE English with GCSE Media grades.

| English GCSE Grades | Media GCSE Grades | | | | | | | | | Total |
|---|---|---|---|---|---|---|---|---|---|---|
| | 9 | 8 | 7 | 6 | 5 | 4 | 3 | 2 | 1 | |
| 9 | | | | | | | | | | |
| 8 | | 2 | 2 | 3 | | | | | | 7 |
| 7 | | 1 | 3 | 4 | | | | 1 | | 9 |
| 6 | | | 8 | 10 | 6 | 1 | | | | 25 |
| 5 | | | | 1 | | 2 | | | | 3 |
| 4 | | | | | | | | 1 | | 1 |
| 3 | | | | | | | | | | |
| 2 | | | | | | | | | | |
| 1 | | | | | | | | | | |
| Total | | 3 | 13 | 18 | 6 | 3 | | 2 | | 45 |

The percentage of pupils who received a Level 5 in Media is approximately what? To the nearest whole number.

Answer [                    ]

## Question 15

Below is a stem and leaf diagram showing the finishing time, in seconds, of 15 sprinters who took part in a race.

| | | | | | | |
|---|---|---|---|---|---|---|
| 1 | 8 | 9 | | | | |
| 2 | 0 | 4 | 5 | 6 | 6 | 9 |
| 3 | 1 | 3 | 5 | 9 | | |
| 4 | 0 | 3 | 4 | | | |
| 5 | | | | | | |

What is the median finishing time?

Answer [          ]

## Question 16

Using the above stem and leaf diagram, what is the mean finishing time? To one decimal point.

Answer [          ]

## Question 17

A ruler is 30 cm in length, correct to the nearest centimetre. What is the smallest possible length of the ruler?

Answer [          ]

## Question 18

The head of English created the following table showing the number of pupils in each year group who got a Level 4 or above in their test.

What is the percentage of pupils in all the year groups combined that got a Level 4 or above in their test? Give your answer to the nearest whole number.

| Year Group | No. of pupils | No. of pupils who achieved a Level 4 or above in their English Test |
|:---:|:---:|:---:|
| 7 | 86 | 56 |
| 8 | 93 | 48 |
| 9 | 102 | 72 |
| 10 | 99 | 52 |
| 11 | 106 | 85 |
| 12 | 68 | 56 |

Answer [        ]

## Question 19

Add $\frac{7}{9}$ of 189 to $\frac{5}{8}$ of 128.

Answer [        ]

## Question 20

Responses when asked how they get to school

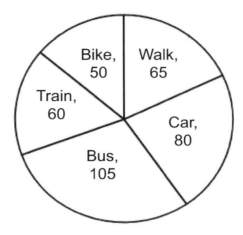

Among the respondents, 85% of the people who said they walk to school and 90% of the people who said they bike to school also said that there school was less than 5 miles away. How many people said that they walk or bike to school because it is less than 5 miles away? Rounded to the nearest whole number.

| A | B | C | D | E |
|---|---|---|---|---|
| 50 | 100 | 120 | 125 | 145 |

*ANSWERS TO NUMERICAL REASONING*

Q1. D = 16.4

EXPLANATION = to work out the percentage overall total that was sold in April, divide how many bikes were sold in April (189) by the total (1149) and then multiply it by 100. (189 ÷ 1149 x 100 = 16.4).

Q2. A = 15.7%

EXPLANATION = to work out the overall percentage total that was sold to France, divide how many bikes were sold to France (180) by the total (1149) and then multiply it by 100. (180 ÷ 1149 x 100 = 15.66). Rounded up to 1 decimal place = 15.7.

Q3. D = 38

EXPLANATION = to work out the average number of units per month imported to Brazil over the first 4 months of the year, you add up the first 4 amounts (Jan-April) and then divide it by how many numbers there are (4). So, (42 + 41 + 37 + 32 = 152 ÷ 4 = 38).

Q4. B = February

EXPLANATION = to work out the biggest increase in total sales from the previous month, you work out the difference between the totals for each of the months and work out which has the biggest increase. Between January and February, there was an increase by 19. None of the other months have a bigger increase and therefore February is the correct answer.

Q5. C = 33.5

EXPLANATION = nylon material = 34 + 32 + 36 + 28 + 40 + 31 = 201 ÷ 6 = 33.5.

Q6. A = 15

EXPLANATION = to work out the range, find the smallest and highest number of polyester imports (18) and (33) So, 33 – 18 = 15 (thousands).

Q7. E = 2

EXPLANATION = to work out the difference, add up the first 3 months for cotton (38 + 22 + 40 = 100). Add up the first 3 months for nylon (34 + 32 + 36 = 102). So, the difference between cotton and nylon = 102 – 100 = 2 (thousands).

Q8. B = 94:130

EXPLANATION = 94,000:130,000. Divide both numbers by 1000 to give you 94:130.

Q9. 12 : 13

EXPLANATION = the ratio of girls to boys is 60:65. However, both sides of this ratio are divisible by 5. Dividing by 5 gives 12:13. 13 has no common factors (apart from 1). So the simplest form of the ratio is 12:13. This means there are 12 girls in the lunch hall for every 13 boys.

Q10. E = 36 and 45

EXPLANATION = this is a triangular number sequence. It uses the pattern of the number of dots which forms a triangle. By adding another row of dots (which increases by 1 each time) and counting all the dots, we can find the next number of the sequence.

Q11. Your box and whisper plot diagram should look like this:

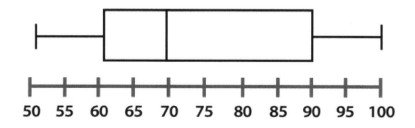

Q12. 14

EXPLANATION = the lower quartile range is the first line the forms the box. So, the correct answer would be 14.


Q13. 67.2%

EXPLANATION = add up the "number of pupils multiplied by media mock exam" and then divide it by the "number of pupils".

| Media mock exam (%) | No. of pupils | No. of pupils X media mock exam (%) |
|---|---|---|
| 10 | 0 | 10 X 0 = 0 |
| 20 | 2 | 20 X 2 = 40 |
| 30 | 3 | 30 X 3 = 90 |
| 40 | 6 | 40 X 6 = 240 |
| 50 | 8 | 50 X 8 = 400 |
| 60 | 11 | 60 X 11 = 660 |
| 70 | 8 | 70 X 8 = 560 |
| 80 | 15 | 80 X 15 = 1,200 |
| 90 | 12 | 90 X 12 = 1,080 |
| 100 | 3 | 100 X 3 = 300 |
| Totals | 68 | |

So, 4570 ÷ 68 = 67.2%.

Q14. 13%

EXPLANATION = number of pupils who received a Level 5 in Media = 6.

Total number of pupils = 45.

So, 6 ÷ 45 x 100 = 13.333%. To the nearest whole number = 13%.

Q15. 29 seconds

EXPLANATION = 'median' simply means 'middle'. So, what number is in the middle? Using the data in ascending order, you will notice that 29 (seconds) is the median/middle number.

Q16. 30.1 seconds

EXPLANATION = to work out the mean number, add up all the numbers and then divide it by how many numbers there are.

So, $452 \div 15 = 30.133$. To one decimal point = 30.1.

Q17. 29.5 cm

EXPLANATION = if 29.5 is rounded up to the nearest whole number, it becomes 30cm. If the number is less than 29.5, like 29.4, it would be rounded down to 29cm. Therefore, 29.5cm is the smallest possible length the ruler can be.

Q18. 67%

EXPLANATION = add up total number of pupils = 554.

Add up the number of pupils who achieved a Level 4 or above in English = 369.

To work out the overall percentage = $369 \div 554 \times 100 = 66.6\%$.

To the nearest whole number = 67%.

Q19. 227

EXPLANATION = $189 \div 9 \times 7 = 147$.

$128 \div 8 \times 5 = 80$.

So, $80 + 147 = 227$.

Q20. B = 100

EXPLANATION = first you need to work out the percentage of the people who walked = 85% of 65 = 65 ÷ 100 x 85 = 55.25.

Now, you need to work out the percentage of the people who biked = 90% of 50 = 50 ÷ 100 x 90 = 45.

So, 55.25 + 45 = 100.25. Rounded to the nearest whole number = 100.

## Inductive Reasoning

Inductive Reasoning has become a popular screening process, used by a lot of employers to provide the employer with valuable information in regards to the way that people think or react.

This test solely measures your ability to solve problems. These tests are designed to measure logical reasoning and perpetual reasoning skills. The skills that you need to demonstrate in an Inductive Reasoning test are transferable to most job roles, specifically to jobs involving engineering, science, IT or software development. The police want to see candidates who show acute awareness and understanding of logical thinking and reasoning ability.

### What are Inductive Reasoning Tests?

Inductive Reasoning tests are similar to 'Diagrammatic' or 'Abstract' Reasoning tests, where the test requires you to identify patterns or consistencies amongst sets of objects, shapes or words.  It is common for Inductive Reasoning Tests to present matrices of shapes and objects to highlight patterns and similarities, in order to visualise what is happening as a sequence progresses. These tests are a form of aptitude assessment, which examine logical and methodical understanding.

It is often said that people who perform to a high standard in these tests, tend to have higher levels of capacity in regards to thinking conceptually and analytically; and draw upon patterns and configurations.

### What to expect

Inductive Reasoning tests provide a series of diagrams, of which there will be an underlying rule affecting the layout. Your job is to identify what is happening in the diagrams, to determine the pattern of the sequence.

Typically, in an Inductive Reasoning test, you will need to choose between 4-6 possible answers. It is important that you understand the pattern of the sequence before choosing your answer. The answers will all look very similar; and at first glance, may seem like the correct answer. However, if you have not distinguished the correct pattern or rule that is recurring, chances are you will not choose the correct answer.

The time limit for these tests is often quite limited. Thus, many candidates find it difficult to complete the test in the time provided. We cannot stress enough that these tests are merely used to decipher whether or not you are rightly suitable for a job role. Therefore, employers are not looking for you to complete the whole test, they are looking at your accurate results, as well as efficiency.

## Aims for Inductive Reasoning

For psychometric testing, you need to aim for speed as well as accuracy. It is important to be able to undergo these tests with the utmost confidence and composure, in order to work swiftly and effectively.

The only way to prepare for an Inductive Reasoning test, or any other form of psychometric testing, is simply through practising. Any psychometric test requires you to be familiar with the concept and layout of the test, which you will need to have to stand any chance of successfully passing. Practising will no doubt maximise your potential and increase your performance, meaning your chances of success will improve dramatically.

In order to succeed, you need to have a clear understanding of the principles and purpose of the test. You need to know what to expect and how to complete the questions, so it doesn't startle you on the day of your real test.

Also, practising beforehand will give you some indication of how well you will perform these tests under severe time constraints. As mentioned earlier, the test is set under extreme time limits; practice will not only enable you to determine how well you perform under these time limits, but also help to improve your logical ability and timing skills.

## What do the questions look like?

The types of questions that you will face in the Inductive Reasoning test will vary depending on the type of test you are sitting. However, this book provides you with a variety of sample questions and explanations in order to give you a clear understanding of what to expect.

The aim of Inductive Reasoning tests is to determine how well you can understand and visualise information to solve problems. You need to be able to recognise and identify patterns amongst abstract shapes and images.

Inductive Reasoning includes questions regarding:

• Rotations;

• Reflections;

• Alternations;

• Translations;

• Replacements;

• 3D shapes.

In order for you to gain the best knowledge and practice, the following testing section will include a variety of question types, to ensure you are fully prepared for any Inductive Reasoning test that you may be required to sit.


Now, let's take a look at some sample practice questions, before we move onto a practice test!

## Sequences

*Work out which figure come next in the sequence.*

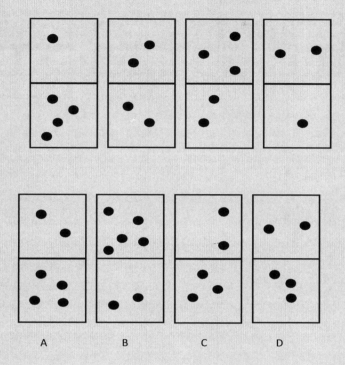

### How to work it out

* The answer would be A. Starting from the first diagram in the top box, as it moves along the sequence it follows the pattern of 1, 2, 3... swapping from top to bottom box.

* Starting with the bottom part of the diagram, swapping from bottom to top box it follows the pattern 4, 2, 2, 2...

### Answer

A

## Odd One Out

*Find the odd one out.*

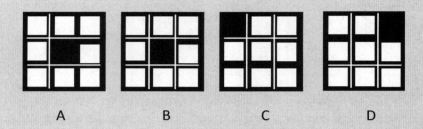

A         B         C         D

### How to work it out

- Pay attention to everything that is going on: colours, patterns, position, shapes etc.

- You should notice that figures A, C and D all contain three lines, whereas figure B contains four lines and therefore makes it the odd one out.

### Answer

B

## Complete the Series

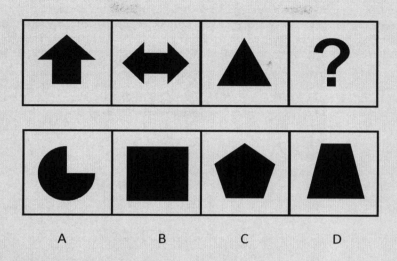

## How to work it out

- Pay attention to symmetry, shades, shapes, size, patterns etc.

- You should notice that the first shape has one line of symmetry, the second has two, and the third has three.

- So you need a shape with four lines of symmetry to complete the series. Figure B (the square) has four lines of symmetry, therefore this is the correct answer.

## Answer

B

## Rotating Shapes

*Which answer option, if rotated, would look like the question figure?*

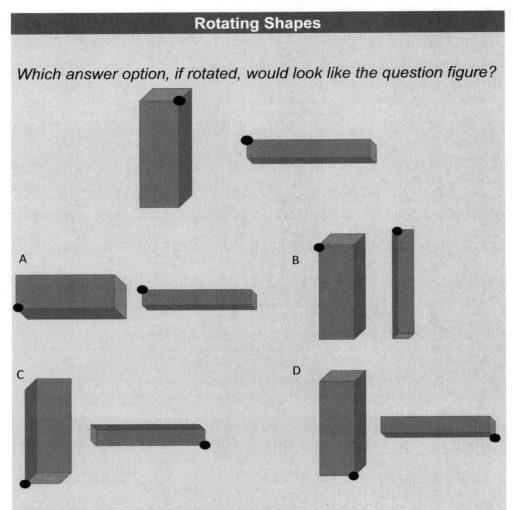

### How to work it out

- To get from the figure shown to option C you would rotate both objects 180 degrees clockwise or anticlockwise.

- REMEMBER = both shapes need to be rotated exactly the same number of times, in the exact same direction.

### Answer

C

## Question 1

What figure completes the sequence pattern?

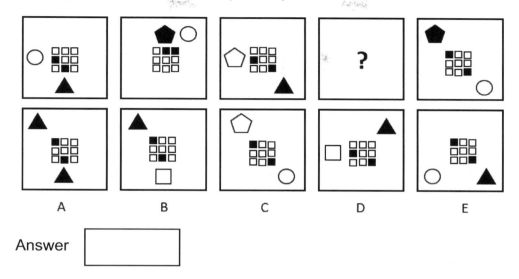

Answer

## Question 2

What figure completes the sequence pattern?

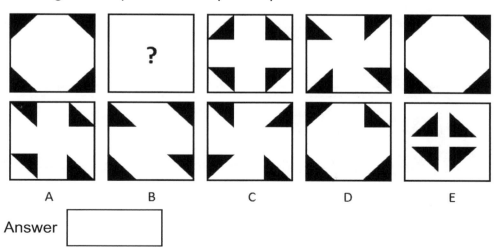

Answer

## Question 3

What figure completes the sequence pattern?

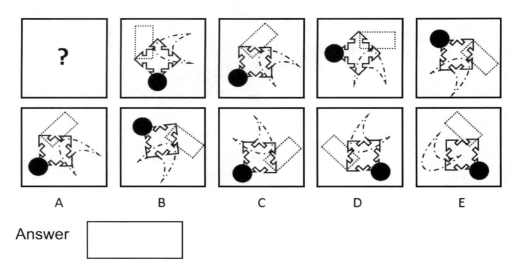

Answer

## Question 4

What figure completes the sequence pattern?

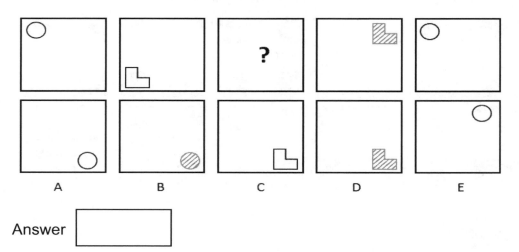

Answer

## Question 5

What figure completes the sequence pattern?

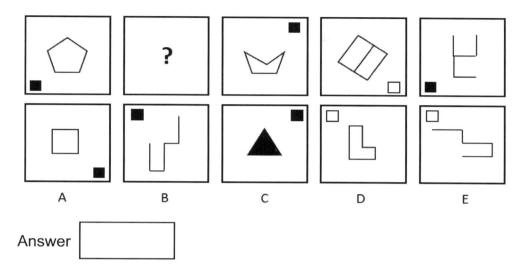

A    B    C    D    E

Answer

## Question 6

What figure completes the sequence pattern?

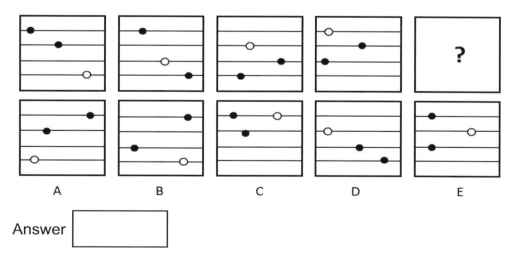

A    B    C    D    E

Answer

## Question 7

What figure completes the sequence pattern?

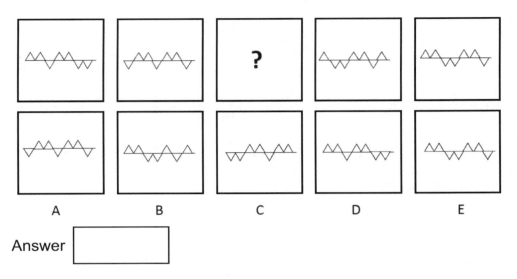

Answer

## Question 8

What figure completes the sequence pattern?

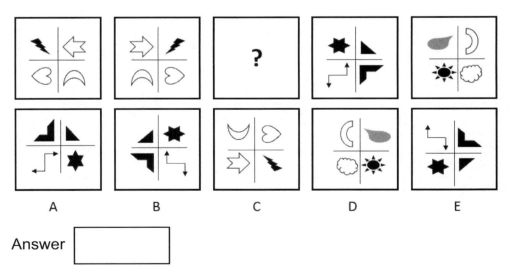

Answer

## Question 9

What figure completes the sequence pattern?

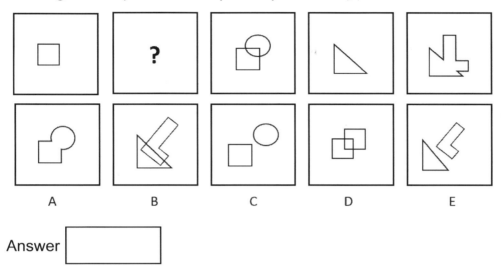

Answer

## Question 10

What figure completes the sequence pattern?

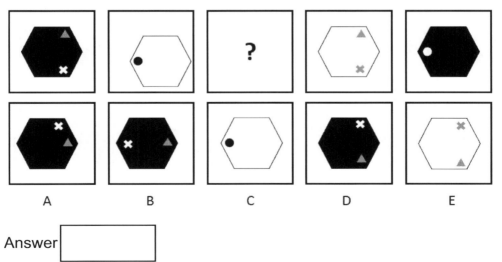

Answer

## Question 11

What figure completes the sequence pattern?

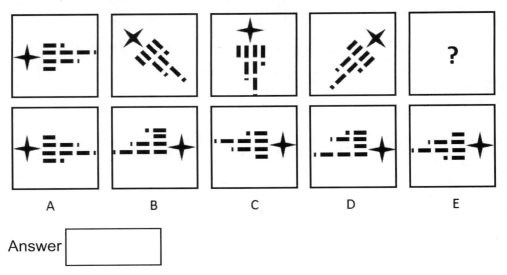

Answer [ ]


## Question 12

What figure completes the sequence pattern?

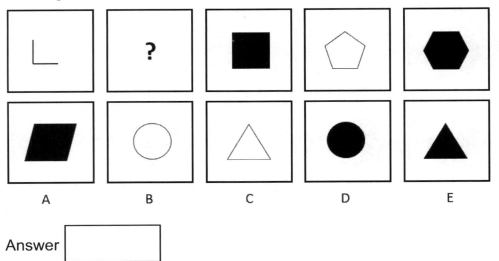

Answer [ ]

## Question 13

What figure completes the sequence pattern?

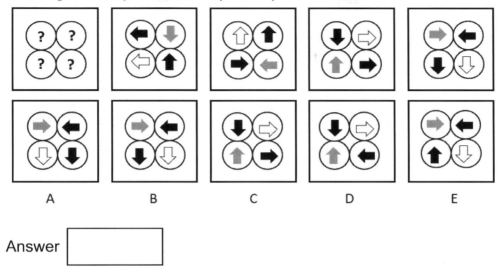

Answer

## Question 14

What figure completes the sequence pattern?

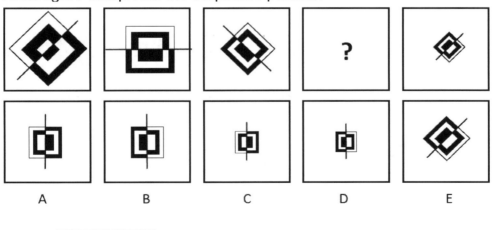

Answer

## Question 15

What figure fits in with the sequence pattern?

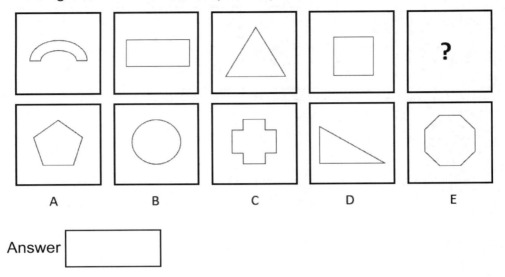

Answer [          ]

## Question 16

What figure completes the sequence pattern?

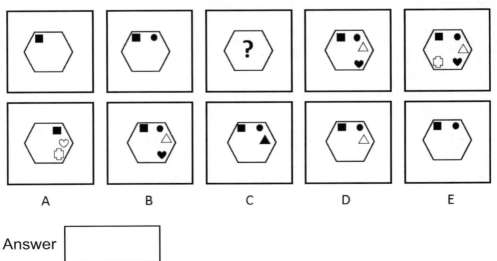

Answer [          ]

## Question 17

What figure completes the sequence pattern?

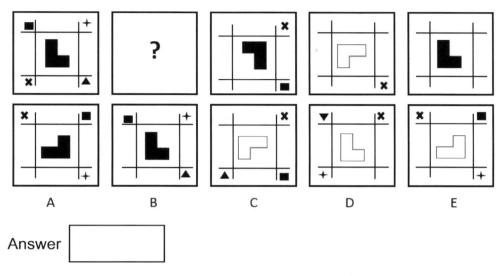

| A | B | C | D | E |

Answer

## Question 18

What figure fits in with the sequence pattern?

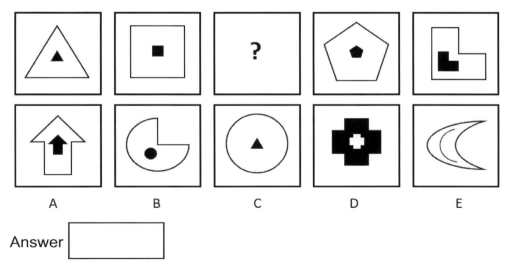

| A | B | C | D | E |

Answer

## Question 19

What figure completes the sequence pattern?

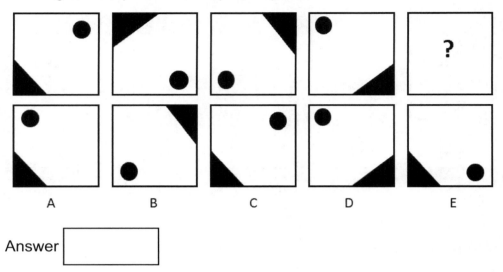

Answer

## Question 20

What figure completes the sequence pattern?

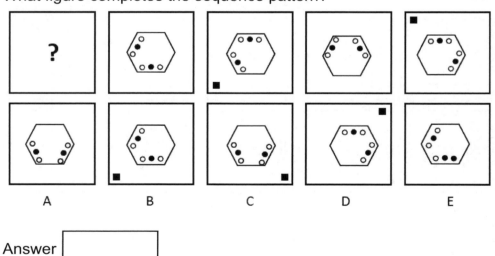

Answer

## ANSWERS TO INDUCTIVE REASONING

### Q1. B

Rule 1 = the large shape's position is determined by the small, black squares.

Rule 2 = for the large shapes; one shape has to be white, and the other has to be black.

Figure A can be ruled out because both the large shapes are black; there should be one large shape that is white. Figure C can be ruled out because both the large shapes are white; there should be one large shape that is black. Figure D can be ruled out because the black triangle should be positioned at the bottom right corner (the small black square determines the place of the large shape). Figure E can be ruled out because the white circle should be positioned at the top left corner (the small black square determines the place of the large shape).

### Q2. C

Rule 1 = each shaded triangle has been rotated 90° clockwise.

Figure A can be ruled out because the triangle in the top right corner needs to be rotated 90° anti-clockwise; the triangle in the bottom left corner needs to be rotated 90° anti-clockwise. Figure B can be ruled out because all the triangles have been rotated incorrectly. Figure D can be ruled out because all of the triangles have been rotated incorrectly. Figure E can be ruled out because it is a replica of box 3 in the sequence; it has just been condensed.

### Q3. D

Rule 1 = the whole shape is being rotated 45° clockwise. The figure in box 1 is a 45° rotation into box 2. Box 2 is a 45° rotation into box 3 and so forth.

Figure A can be ruled out because it is a replica of the image in box 2. Figure B can be ruled out because it is a replica of box 5. Figure C can be ruled out because it is a reflection of what the answer *should* be. Figure E can be ruled out because the rectangle and moon-shape have swapped places.

## Q4. B

Rule 1 = the shapes move one corner anti-clockwise as the sequence progresses.

Rule 2 =the shapes alternate from a circle to an 'L' shape.

Rule 3 = the colour pattern alternates from white, white, patterned, patterned and repeats.

Figure A can be ruled out because the circle needs to be shaded as opposed to being white. Figure C can be ruled out because it needs to be a shaded circle as opposed to a white 'L' shape. Figure D can be ruled out because it needs to be a patterned circle as opposed to a patterned 'L' shape. Figure E can be ruled out because the circle needs to be patterned and in the bottom right corner as opposed to the top right corner.

## Q5. E

Rule 1 = the small square moves around one place clockwise as the sequence progresses.

Rule 2 = the small square alternates from black to white as the sequence progresses.

Rule 3 = the shape in the centre must contain 5 sides.

Figure A can be ruled out because the shape in the centre has only 4 sides; also, the black square in the bottom right corner should be a white square in the top left corner. Figure B can be ruled out because the black square needs to be a white square. Figure C can be ruled out because the shape in the centre needs to be five sides; also the black square in the top right corner needs to be a white square in the top left corner. Figure D can be ruled out because the shape in the centre has six sides, and it should have five sides.

## Q6. A

Rule 1 = the two black dots remain straight after one another (there is no line in between the two black dots).

Rule 2 = the white dot remains one line ahead of the last black dot.

Rule 3 = the dots move up one line each time.

Figure B can be ruled out because the black dots should not have a line in between them. Figure C can be ruled out because the black dot should not be on the same line as the white dot. Figure D can be ruled out because the white dot needs to be on the bottom line. Figure E can be ruled out because the two black dots have been separated by the white dot in the middle.

## Q7. C

Rule 1 = the triangles move one place to the right as the sequence progresses.

Rule 2 = once the triangle reaches the end of the horizontal line, the triangle is placed back at the start.

Figure A can be ruled out because it is a replica of box 2. Figure B can be ruled out because the triangles at the end of the figure are incorrect. Figure D can be ruled out because it is a replica of box 1. Figure E can be ruled out because it is a replica of box 5.

## Q8. B

Rule 1 = the sequence is all about vertical reflections.

Rule 2 = box 1 is reflected to box 2. Box 3 is reflected to box 4 and so on.

Figure A can be ruled out because this has been reflected and then rotated; it is not a mere reflection of the next box. Figure C can be ruled out because this is a horizontal reflection of box 2; we want a reflection of box 4. Figure D can be ruled out because this is a vertical reflection of box 5; we want a vertical reflection of box 4. Figure E can be ruled out because this is a horizontal reflection of box 4; we want a vertical reflection of box 4.

## Q9. A

Rule 1 = to get from box 1 to box 2, the shapes need to merge. It uses one shape (in box 1); and you have to work out which shape it is being merged with (in this case it is a square and a circle). The third box indicates which two shapes have been merged together and demonstrates the overlap.

Rule 3 = after the first three boxes, the sequence begins again, with different shapes; but following the same rule.

Figure B can be ruled out because the shapes merging together need to be a square and a circle. Figure C can be ruled out because two shapes need to be merged as opposed to separate. Figure D can be ruled out because the two shapes need to be a circle and a square; and not two squares. Figure E can be ruled out because the shapes need to be a circle and a square; not a triangle and an 'L' shape.

## Q10. D

Rule 1 = the large hexagon alternates between black and white as the sequence progresses.

Rule 2 = the grey triangle moves two points anti-clockwise around the hexagon as the sequence progresses.

Rule 3 = the small cross moves two points clockwise around the hexagon as the sequence progresses.

Rule 4 = if the triangle and the cross coincide, the shapes become a black circle (if on a white hexagon) or a white circle (if on a black hexagon).

Figures A, B, C and E all have one or more shapes in the incorrect position and therefore cannot follow the sequence.

## Q11. E

Rule 1 = the whole shape is being rotated 45° clockwise. The figure in box 1 is a 45° rotation into box 2. Box 2 is a 45° rotation into box 3 and so forth.

Figure A can be ruled out because it is a horizontal reflection of box A. Figure B can be ruled out because the line on the top should be at the bottom. Figure C can be ruled out because it is a vertical reflection of box A. Figure D can be ruled out because the lines have been positioned in different places.

## Q12. C

Rule 1 = the sequence adds one side to the previous shape, as the sequence progresses. For example a triangle (3 sides), turns into a square (4 sides) and so forth.

Rule 2 = the sequence alternates colour pattern between black and white.

Figure A can be ruled out because the shape needs to be 3-sided, not 4-sided. Figure B can be ruled out because the shape needs to be 3-sided, not a circle. Figure D can be ruled out because the shape needs to be 3-sided and white, not a circle and black. Figure E can be ruled out because it needs to be a white triangle, not a black triangle.

## Q13. B

Rule 1 = the whole shape rotates 90° clockwise.

Figure A can be ruled out because the white and black arrows pointing downwards have swapped places. Figure C can be ruled out because this is a replica of box 4. Figure D can be ruled out because none of the arrows are in the correct position. Figure E can be ruled out because the black arrow pointing upwards should be pointing downwards.

## Q14. B

Rule 1 = the whole shape is being rotated 45° clockwise. The figure in box 1 is a 45° rotation into box 2. Box 2 is a 45° rotation into box 3 and so forth.

Rule 2 = each figure gets smaller than the previous.

Figure A can be ruled out because it is a reflection of what the answer *should* look like. Figure C can be ruled out because it is the wrong size and has been reflected. Figure D can be ruled out because it is the wrong size. Figure E can be ruled out because it should only be rotated 45° from the previous box (instead it has been rotated an extra 45°).

## Q15. A

Rule 1 = each shape adds another line of symmetry. For example, the first shape (the rainbow shape) has 1 line of symmetry, the second shape (the rectangle) has 2 lines of symmetry and so forth.

Figure B can be ruled out because a circle will look the same no matter how many times you rotate it. Figure C can be ruled out because it has 4 lines of symmetry. Figure D can be ruled out because this triangle has no line of symmetry. Figure E can be ruled out because this has 8 lines of symmetry.

## Q16. D

Rule 1 = in each of the corners of the hexagon, a shape is placed.

Rule 2 = these shapes start in the top left corner and are added in a clockwise manner.

Figure A can be ruled out because we are looking for a black square, a black circle and a white triangle. Figure B can be ruled out because we only need three shapes, not four. Figure C can be ruled out because the triangle needs to be white, not black. Figure E can be ruled out because we need three shapes, not two.

## Q17. E

Rule 1 = the shape in the middle rotates 90° anti-clockwise as the sequence progresses.

Rule 2 = the shape in the middle alternates from black to white as the sequence progresses.

Rule 3 = the small shapes move one position to the next corner (in a clockwise manner).

Rule 4 = as the shapes rotate around, a shape is left off. You will notice, that the 'cross' shape appears the most, therefore this must be the beginning of this sequence, and so the last shape rotated (using the 'cross' to begin) will be left off.

Figure A can be ruled out because the shape in the middle needs to be white, not black. Figure B can be ruled out because the shape in the middle needs to be white, and rotated 90° anti-clockwise. Also, the small shapes do not follow the correct pattern. Figure C can be ruled out because the shape in the middle needs to be rotated 180°. Also the small shapes do not follow the correct pattern. Figure D can be ruled out because the shape in the middle needs to be rotated 90° anti-clockwise. None of the small shapes are in the correct position.

## Q18. A

Rule 1 = the large shape is white. The small shapes are black.

Rule 2 = the small shape inside the large shape is the **same** shape.

Figure B can be ruled out because the 'pac-man' shape does not contain the same shape in the centre of the shape, it contains a circle instead. Figure C can be ruled out because the large white circle should contain a small black circle, not a black triangle. Figure D can be ruled out because the large shape should be white, and the small shape should be black. Figure E can be ruled out because the moon shape only contains a curved line, not a small moon shape.

## Q19. C

Rule 1 = the shapes move 90° clockwise as the sequence progresses.

Figure A can be ruled out because the black dot should be in the top right corner, not the top left. Figure B can be ruled out because the black dot and black triangle should be in one another's place. Figure D can be ruled out because the dot and the triangle need to be moved one corner clockwise. Figure E can be ruled out because the black dot needs to be in the top right corner, not the bottom right.

## Q20. C

Rule 1 = the dots move to one side in a clockwise motion.

Rule 2 = every other figure in the sequence contains a black square in the corner of the whole box. This square moves one corner clockwise.

Figure A can be ruled out because the figure does not contain a black square in the bottom right corner. Figure B can be ruled out because the dots are not in the correct position. They need to be positioned so that the side that is empty and in between the two lines of dots is at the bottom. The black square should be in the bottom right corner, not the bottom left. Figure D can be ruled out because the side that is empty and in between the two lines of dots should be at the bottom, not at the top right side. The black square should be in the bottom right corner, not the top right. Figure E can be ruled out because the side that is empty and in between the two lines of dots should be at the bottom, not bottom left. The figure also needs to contain a black square in the bottom right corner.

# THE POLICE INSPECTOR COMPETENCY INTERVIEW

The final stage of the assessment centre is a competency-based structured interview. The interview will last for 30 minutes, and consist of 6 questions in total. The questions in the interview will focus upon your previous experience, and your ability to deal with future challenges. You will be scored against how well your responses match with the police inspector core competencies.

In this chapter, we'll provide you with all of the information that you could possibly need, on how to ace this interview.

Under normal circumstances the interview board will consist of two or three people. These can be from either the uniformed side of the service or support staff. It is important to remember that whilst you will be nervous, you should try not to let this get in the way of your success. In general, police inspectors are confident people who have the ability to rise to a challenge and perform under difficult and pressurised situations. Treat the interview no differently to this. You ARE capable of becoming a police inspector, and the nerves that you have on the day are only natural, in fact they will help you to perform better if you have prepared sufficiently. The crucial element to your success, as with the rest of the selection process, is your preparation.

The interview board will have a number of set questions to choose from. Although these are constantly changing, they will usually form part of the police inspector core competencies.

Before attending your interview, ensure that you read, digest and understand the core competencies and behavioural expectations. Without these it will be difficult to pass the interview.

The interviewers will give you 5 minutes to answer each question. Once the five minutes is up, you will be stopped, and immediately move onto the next question. The interviewers will ask you to correlate a previous experience you have had, or an action that you have taken, with one of the core competencies. For example, you might be asked:

*'Give us an example of a time when you have demonstrated your integrity.'*

When you respond to this question, you need to use the STAR method that we outlined earlier in this guide. Since these are competency-based questions, you will need to provide a structured and lengthy response, that covers everything the assessors are looking for.

## Preparing For The Interview

When preparing for the competency-based interview you should try to formulate responses to questions that surround the assessable core competencies.

The responses that you provide should be specific examples of where you have been in that particular scenario.

In your 'Welcome Pack', which will be sent to you approximately 2 weeks before the date of your assessment centre, you should find examples of the 'core competencies' relevant to a police inspector. These are the criteria that you will be scored against so it is worthwhile reading them beforehand and trying to structure your answers around them as best you can.

For example, one of the sections you will be assessed against could be "Integrity'. Now, there are two ways in which this could be done. The assessor may ask you flat out, 'Please give an example of a time where you have demonstrated your integrity.' Alternatively, they might ask you something like 'Please provide an example of a time when you have taken responsibility to solve a problem.' While this question doesn't directly ask you to 'demonstrate your integrity', you will need to demonstrate as many of the competencies as you can in your response. You might also be asked a question where you have to give an example of where you worked effectively as part of a team in order to achieve a difficult task or goal. Try to think of an example where you have had to do this and structure your answer around the core competencies required, e.g. you worked cooperatively with the others, supported the rest of the team members and persuaded them to follow your ideas for completing the task.

On the following page we have provided you with an example of how your response could be structured. Remember that the following sample question and response is for example purposes only:

> **Question – Please provide an example of where you have taken responsibility to resolve a problem?**

*"After reading an appeal in my local paper from a local charity, I decided to try to raise money for this worthwhile cause by organising a charity car wash day at the local school during the summer holidays. I decided that the event would take place in a month's time, which would*

*give me enough time to organise such an event. The head teacher at the school agreed to support me during the organisation of the event and provided me with the necessary resources required to make it a success.*

*I set about organising the event and soon realised that I had made a mistake in trying to arrange everything on my own, so I arranged for two of my work colleagues to assist me.*

*Once they had agreed to help me I started out by providing them with a brief of what I wanted them to do. I informed them that, in order for the event to be a success, we needed to act with integrity and professionalism at all times. I then asked one of them to organise the booking of the school and arrange local sponsorship in the form of buckets, sponges and car wash soap to use on the day, so that we did not have to use our own personal money to buy them. I asked the second person to arrange advertising in the local newspaper and radio stations so that we could let the local community know about our charity car wash event, which would in turn hopefully bring in more money on the day for the charity.*

*Following a successful advertising campaign, I was inundated with calls from local newspapers about our event and it was becoming hard work having to keep talking to them and explaining what the event was all about. But I knew that this information was important if we were to raise our target of £500.*

*Everything was going well right up to the morning of the event, when I realised we had not got the key to open the school gates. It was the summer holidays so the caretaker was not there to open the gates for us. Not wanting to let everyone down, I jumped in my car and made my way down to the caretaker's house and managed to wake him up and get the key just in time before the car wash event was due to start. In the end, the day was a great success and we all managed to raise £600 for the local charity.*

*Throughout the event I put in lots of extra effort in order to make it a great success. Once the event was over, I decided to ask the head teacher for feedback on how he thought I had managed the project.*

*He provided me with some excellent feedback and some good pointers for how I might improve in the future when organising events. I took on-board his feedback in order to improve my skills."*

The answer above has hopefully highlighted the importance of matching the core competencies and key behaviours that are being assessed.

When you receive your 'Welcome Pack', make sure you read it thoroughly and prepare yourself fully for the interview. Preparation is everything. By reading exactly what is required, you will increase your chances of success on the day.

On the following pages, we have provided you with a number of sample assessment centre interview questions that are based around the core competencies. Following each question we have provided you with some useful tips and advice on how you may consider answering the question.

Once you have read the question and the tips, use the template on the following page to create a response using your own experiences and knowledge.

## SAMPLE COMPETENCY-BASED INTERVIEW QUESTION 1

> Please provide an example of where you have worked as part of a team to achieve a difficult task.

Tips for constructing your response

- Try to think of a situation where you volunteered to work with a team in order to achieve a difficult task. It is better to say that you volunteered as opposed to being asked to get involved by another person;

- Those candidates who can provide an example where they achieved the task despite the constraints of time will generally score better.

Consider structuring your response in the following manner:

**STEP 1** Explain what the situation was and how you became involved.

**STEP 2** Now explain who else was involved and what the task was.

**STEP 3** Explain why the task was difficult and whether there were any time constraints.

**STEP 4** Explain how it was decided who would carry out what task.

**STEP 5** Now explain what had to be done and how you overcame any obstacles or hurdles.

**STEP 6** Explain what the result/outcome was. Try to make the result positive as a result of your actions.

Now use the template on the following page to construct your own response to this question based on your own experiences and knowledge.

**Sample competency-based interview question 1**

Please provide an example of where you have worked as part of a team to achieve a difficult task.

Examples of probing questions:

1. Would you have done anything different next time?

2. How did the end result make you feel?

## SAMPLE COMPETENCY-BASED INTERVIEW QUESTION 2

> Provide an example of where you have challenged someone's behaviour that was either discriminatory or inappropriate.
>
> What did you do and what did you say?

Tips for constructing your response:

- When challenging this type of behaviour, make sure you remain calm at all times and never become aggressive or confrontational.

Consider structuring your response in the following manner:

**STEP 1** Explain what the situation was and how you became involved.

**STEP 2** Now explain who else was involved and why you felt that the behaviour was inappropriate or discriminatory. What was it that was being said or done?

**STEP 3** Now explain what you said or did and why.

**STEP 4** Explain how the other person/people reacted when you challenged the behaviour.

**STEP 5** Now explain what the end result was. Try to make the result positive following your actions.

**STEP 6** Finally explain why you think it was that the people/ person behaved as they did.

Now use the template on the following page to construct your own response to this question based on your own experiences and knowledge.

**Sample competency-based interview question 2**

Provide an example of where you have challenged someone's behaviour that was either discriminatory or inappropriate. What did you do and what did you say?

Examples of probing questions:

1. How did you feel when you were challenging their behaviour?

2. How did the person or people react when you challenged their behaviour?

## SAMPLE COMPETENCY-BASED INTERVIEW QUESTION 3

> Provide an example of where you have helped somebody from a different culture or background to your own. What did you do and what did you say?

Tips for constructing your response:

- Try to think of a situation where you have gone out of your way to help somebody;

- Try to demonstrate your belief in equality and fairness.

Consider structuring your response in the following manner:

**STEP 1** Explain what the situation was and how you became involved. It is better to say that you volunteered to be involved rather than to say that you were asked to.

**STEP 2** Now explain who else was involved and why they needed your help or assistance.

**STEP 3** Now explain what you said or did and why. Also explain any factors you took into consideration when helping them.

**STEP 4** Explain how the other person/people reacted to your help or assistance. Did they benefit from it?

**STEP 5** Now explain what the end result was. Try to make the result positive following your actions.

Now use the template on the following page to construct your own response to this question based on your own experiences and knowledge.

**Sample competency-based interview question 3**

Provide an example of where you have helped somebody from a different culture or background to your own. What did you do and what did you say?

Examples of probing questions:

1. What did you learn from this experience?

2. Would you have done anything differently?

## SAMPLE COMPETENCY-BASED INTERVIEW QUESTION 4

> Provide an example of where you have solved a difficult problem. What did you do?

- Explain through your thought process, giving clear steps as to how you reached your decision;

- Explain how your thought process led to you solving the problem.

Consider structuring your response in the following manner:

**STEP 1** Explain what the situation was and why the problem was difficult.

**STEP 2** Now explain what action you took in order to solve the difficult problem.

**STEP 3** Now explain why you took that particular action, and also the thought process behind your actions.

**STEP 4** Explain the barriers or difficulties that you had to overcome.

**STEP 5** Now explain what the end result was. Try to make the result positive following your actions.

Now use the template on the following page to construct your own response to this question based on your own experiences and knowledge.

**Sample competency-based interview question 4**

Provide an example of where you have solved a difficult problem. What did you do?

Examples of probing questions:

1.  What did you learn from this experience?

2.  Could you have done it any better?

## SAMPLE COMPETENCY-BASED INTERVIEW QUESTION 5

> Provide an example of where you have broken down barriers between a group of people.

Tips for constructing your response:

- Read carefully the core competency that relates to serving the public.

Try to include keywords and phrases from the core competency in your response to this question, such as:

1. "I tried to understand each person's needs and concerns."

2. "I took steps to identify the best way that we could all work together."

3. "I had their best interests at heart throughout."

4. "I built confidence in them by talking to them."

Consider structuring your response in the following manner:

**STEP 1** Explain what the situation was and why you needed to break down the barriers.

**STEP 2** Now explain what steps you took in order to achieve the goal.

**STEP 3** Now explain why you took that particular action, and also the thought process behind your actions.

**STEP 4** Explain the barriers or difficulties that you had to overcome in order to achieve the task/objective.

**STEP 5** Now explain what the end result was. Try to make the result positive following your actions.

Now use the template on the following page to construct your own response to this question based on your own experiences and knowledge.

**Sample competency-based interview question 5**

Provide an example of where you have broken down barriers between a group of people.

Examples of probing questions:

1. What did you learn from this experience and would you do anything differently next time?

2. What did the other people think about what you did? Were they happy with your work?

## SAMPLE COMPETENCY-BASED INTERVIEW QUESTION 6

> Please provide an example of where you have organised a difficult task effectively.

Tips for constructing your response:

- Try to show how your organisation led to the task being solved;
- Give examples of how you managed the task, in easy steps and stages.

Consider structuring your response in the following manner:

**STEP 1** Explain what the situation was and what it was you needed to organise.

**STEP 2** Now explain why the task was so difficult.

**STEP 3** Now explain what you did and why you did it. Also explain your considerations when organising the task.

**STEP 4** Explain what problems you had and how you overcame them.

**STEP 5** Finally explain what the end result was. Try to provide a positive outcome to the situation.

Now use the template on the following page to construct your own response to this question based on your own experiences and knowledge.

**Sample competency-based interview question 6**

Please provide an example of where you have organised a difficult task effectively.

Examples of probing questions:

1. What did you learn from this experience and would you do anything differently next time?

2. Why do you think the task was so difficult?

## SAMPLE COMPETENCY-BASED INTERVIEW QUESTION 7

> Tell me about a time when you changed how you did something, in response to feedback from someone else.

Tips for creating your response:

- What did you need to develop?

- What feedback did you receive and from whom?

- What steps did you take to improve yourself or someone else?

- What did you specifically say or do?

- What was the result?

### Strong response

Police inspectors receive feedback from their superiors on a regular basis. In their quest to continually improve, the Police Service will invest time, finances and resources into your development. Part of the learning process includes being able to accept feedback and also being able to improve as a result of it. Strong performing candidates will be able to provide a specific example of where they have taken feedback from an employer or otherwise, and used it to improve themselves.

### Weak response

Those candidates who are unable to accept feedback from others and change as a result will generally provide a weak response to this type of question. They will fail to grasp the importance of feedback and in particular where it lies in relation to continuous improvement. Their response will be generic in nature and there will be no real substance or detail to their answer.

### Sample response:

*"During my last appraisal, my line manager identified that I needed to improve in a specific area. I work as a call handler for a large independent communications company. Part of my role involves answering a specific number of calls per hour. If I do not reach my target, then this does not allow the company to meet its standards. I found that I was falling behind on the number of calls answered and this was identified during the appraisal. I needed to develop my skills*

*in the manner in which I handled the call. My line manager played back a number of recorded calls that I had dealt with and it was apparent that I was taking too long speaking to the customer about issues that were irrelevant to the call itself. Because I am a conscientious and caring person I found myself asking the customer how they were and what kind of day they were having.*

*Despite the customers being more than pleased with my level of customer care, this approach was not helping the company and therefore I needed to change my approach. I immediately took on board the comments of my line manager and also took up the offer of development and call handling training. After the training, which took two weeks to complete, I was meeting my targets with ease. In turn, this helped the company to reach its call handling targets."*

Now prepare your own response to this question!

**Sample competency-based interview question 7**

Tell me about a time when you changed how you did something in response to feedback from someone else.

Examples of probing questions:

1.  How did you feel when the feedback was being given?

2.  What, if anything, did you find difficult about making the necessary improvements?

## MORE SAMPLE QUESTIONS TO PREPARE FOR BASED ON THE ASSESSABLE CORE COMPETENCIES

In this short section, we will provide you with a number of other sample interview questions to prepare for:

Q. Give an example of when you have worked towards an organisation's objectives or priorities.

Q. Give an example of when you have planned and organised a difficult task.

Q. Give an example of when you have carried out many different tasks at once.

Q. Give me an example of when you have sought advice from others whilst carrying out a difficult work-related task.

Q. Give an example of when you have provided excellent customer service.

Q. Give me an example of when you have addressed someone else's needs or expectations.

Q. Give me an example of when you have broken down barriers amongst a group of people.

Q. Give an example of when you have worked with another person or group of people to deliver an excellent level of service.

Q. Give an example of when you have worked in accordance with an organisations standards or ethics.

Q. Give an example of when you have taken ownership of a particular problem.

Q. Give an example of when you have acted on your own initiative to resolve an issue or difficult problem.

Q. Give an example of when you have challenged someone's behaviour, which was discriminatory or inappropriate.

Q. Give an example of when you have acted on feedback which has been supplied by someone else.

Q. Give me an example of when you have resolved a difficult situation in a calm manner.

Q. Give me an example of when you have defused a potentially hostile situation.

Q. Give an example of when you have supported other members of a team.

Q. Give an example of when you have worked with other people to achieve a difficult task.

Q. Give an example of when you have briefed a team in relation to a difficult task which had to be achieved.

Q. Give an example of when you have persuaded a group of people to follow your course of action or plan.

Q. Give an example of when you have treated a person or group of people with dignity and respect.

## HOW TO IMPROVE YOUR SCORES THROUGH EFFECTIVE ORAL COMMUNICATION

Whilst you will not normally be questioned directly in relation to oral communication during the interview, you will be assessed indirectly.

During the assessment centre competency-based interview, the panel will be looking to see how you communicate, and also how you structure your responses to the interview questions.

Consider the following points both during the interview and whilst responding to the interview questions:

- When you walk into the interview room stand up straight and introduce yourself. Be polite and courteous at all times and try to come across in a pleasant manner. The panel will be assessing you as soon as you walk through the door, so make sure you make a positive first impression;

- Do not sit down in the interview chair until you are invited to do so. This is good manners;

- When you sit down in the interview chair, sit up straight and do not fidget or slouch. It is acceptable to use hand gestures when explaining your responses to the questions but don't overdo it, as they can become a distraction;

- Structure your responses to the questions in a logical manner – this is very important. When responding to an interview question, start at the beginning and work your way through in a concise manner, and at a pace that is easy for the panel to listen to;

- Speak clearly and in a tone that is easy for the panel to hear. Be confident in your responses;

- When talking to the panel use eye contact but be careful not to look at them in an intimidating manner;

- Consider wearing some form of formal outfit to the interview, such as a suit. Whilst you will not be assessed on the type of outfit you wear to the interview, it will make you come across in a more professional manner.

**Final golden interview tips:**

- Always provide 'specific' examples to the questions being asked;

- During your responses, try to outline your contributions and also provide evidence of the competency area that is being assessed;

- Speak clearly, use correct English and structure your responses in a logical and concise manner.

# THE FINAL
# INTERVIEW

Candidates who have been successful at the assessment centre will face a short wait, before finding out the good news. Following this, the police will sort successful candidates via the preference list that they made in their application form.

Now, if you are lucky, you will simply be offered a place on the course and a job with the constabulary that was at the top of your list. However, the option exists for the constabulary to meet with you first, to discuss your appointment. If they do opt to do this, then you will be invited to attend what is effectively a 'final interview'. The purpose of the final interview is to allow the service to ask you questions that are outside of the competencies that have been assessed at the assessment centre. In essence it allows the service to find out more about you, your application, your motivations for wanting to become a police inspector, and what you know about the role and the service that you are applying to join. They may also ask you questions that are based around what you might do in a given situation.

The interview panel will normally consist of 2-3 people, and is usually made up of uniformed police officers and also a member of the human resources team. The length of the interview will very much depend on the questions the panel want to ask you and also how long your responses are. In general terms, the interview will normally last for approximately one hour.

## HOW TO PREPARE FOR THE FINAL INTERVIEW

If you have made it this far in the selection process, then you have done tremendously well. The Police Service are certainly interested in giving you a place on the Direct Entry course, but they want to find out more about you first. There are a number of areas that you will need to prepare for, and these are as follows:

1. Interview technique.

2. The reasons why you want to become a police inspector, and what you know about the role.

3. What you know about that particular constabulary.

4. Situational interview questions.

Now that we understand how to prepare for the interview, let us break down each particular section in detail.

## INTERVIEW TECHNIQUE

Many candidates spend little or no time improving or developing their interview technique. It is important that you spend sufficient time on this area, as it will allow your confidence to improve.

The way to improve interview technique is to carry out what we call a mock interview. Mock interviews are where you ask a friend or relative to ask you a number of interview questions under formalised interview conditions. This can be achieved at home across your dining room table, or even whilst sat on the chairs in your living room.

During the mock interview, you should work on your interview technique. The mock interview will also give you a valuable opportunity to try out your responses to a number of sample interview questions that are contained within this guide. It is important that your mock interviewer provides you with constructive feedback. Do not choose somebody who will tell you that you were great, even when you weren't, as this just defeats the whole purpose of a mock interview.

## CARRYING OUT A MOCK INTERVIEW

- Choose a quiet room in the house or at another suitable location;

- Set the room up with a table and two chairs;

- The interviewer then invites you into the room and the interview commences. Don't forget to be polite and courteous to the interviewer, and only sit down when invited to do so;

- When the interviewer asks you the questions, respond to them in a logical manner, and in a tone of voice that can be easily heard;

- Throughout the mock interview, work hard on your technique and style. Sit upright at all times, and look at the interviewer using soft eye contact. Do not fidget or slouch in the interview chair;

- Once the interview is over, ask the interviewer for feedback on your performance;

- Repeat the process at least three times, until you are comfortable with your technique and style of answering.

## THE REASONS WHY YOU WANT TO BECOME A POLICE INSPECTOR AND WHAT YOU KNOW ABOUT THE ROLE

During the final interview, the panel may ask you questions that relate to why you want to become an inspector, and in particular what you know about the role.

---

### Why do you want to become a police inspector?

In the build-up to your interview you need to think carefully about why you want to become a police inspector, and what it is exactly that has attracted you to the role. Those candidates who want to become an inspector so that they can 'catch criminals' and 'ride about in a police car with the blue lights flashing' will score poorly. Only you will know the exact reasons why you want to join the police, but here are some examples of good reasons, and examples of poor reasons.

Good reasons to give:

- To make a difference to your community, make it a safer place and reduce any fear that the public may have;

- To carry out a job that is worthwhile and one that makes a difference;

- The variety of the job and the different challenges that you will face on a day-to-day basis;

- The chance to work with a highly professional team that is committed to achieving the values and principles of the service;

- The opportunity to learn new skills.

Poor reasons to give:

- The pay and pension;

- The leave or holiday that you will get;

- Wearing a uniform, which ultimately means you don't have to pay for your own work clothes;

- Catching criminals and driving a police car.

## What do you know about the role?

After studying this guide, you will know a considerable amount about the role of a police inspector. Before the final interview you must carry out plenty of research into the role and what the service will expect of you as a serving police inspector.

Remember that the role is predominantly based around the core competencies, so be fully familiar with them before you attend the interview. It is also advisable that you study your recruitment literature and also the website of the service you are applying to join.

## What do you know about this constabulary?

During the final interview there is a strong possibility that you will be asked questions that relate to the constabulary who are interviewing you. The following are some typical questions that you might hear, in this category:

Q. What is it that has attracted you to this particular constabulary?

Q. What can you tell me about the structure of this constabulary?

Q. What can you tell me about the geographical area of this Police Service?

Q. Can you tell me how this constabulary is doing in relation to crime reduction?

Q. What crime reduction activities is this constabulary currently involved in?

Q. What is neighbourhood policing and how does this constabulary approach it?

Q. What are the ambitions of this Police Service?

Q. Who are our partners and stakeholders?

In order to prepare for questions that relate to the service you are applying to join, your first port of call is their website. From here you will be able to find out a considerable amount of information about their structure and activities and their success in driving down crime.

You may also wish to consider contacting your local police station and asking if it is possible to talk to a serving inspector about his/her role and the activities that the service are currently engaged in.

Now that we have looked into how to prepare for the final interview, it is time to provide you with a number of sample questions and answers. Please note that the questions provided here are for practice purposes only and are not to be relied upon to be the exact questions that you will be asked during your final interview.

## SAMPLE QUESTION NUMBER 1

> *Tell us why you want to become a police inspector.*

### Sample response

*"I have worked in my current role now for a number of years. I have an excellent employer and enjoy working for them but unfortunately no longer find my job challenging. I understand that the role of a police inspector is both demanding and rewarding, and I believe I have the qualities to thrive in such an environment. I love working under pressure, working as part of a team that is diverse in nature and helping people in difficult situations. The public expectations of the police are very high and I believe I have the right qualities to help the police deliver the right service to the community.*

*I have studied the police core competencies and believe that I have the skills to match them and deliver what they require."*

### Top tips

- Don't be negative about your current or previous employer;

- Be positive, enthusiastic and upbeat in your response;

- Make reference to the core competencies if possible.

## SAMPLE QUESTION NUMBER 2

> *Why did you place this particular constabulary at the top of your list?*

### Sample response

*"I have carried out extensive research into the Police Service and in particular this constabulary. I have been impressed by the level of service it provides. The website provides the community with direct access to a different range of topics and the work that is being carried out through your community wardens is impressive. I have looked at the national and local crime statistics and read many different newspapers and articles.*

*I like this Police Service because of its reputation, and the serving officers that I have spoken to have told me that they get a great deal of job satisfaction from working here."*

### Top tips

- Research the service thoroughly and make reference to particular success stories that they have achieved;

- Be positive, enthusiastic and upbeat in your response;

- Be positive about their service and don't be critical of it, even if you think it needs improving in certain areas.

## SAMPLE QUESTION NUMBER 3

> *What does the role of a police inspector involve?*

### Sample response

*"Before I carried out my research and looked into the role of the police inspector, I had the normal, stereotypical view of an inspector sitting behind a desk and making phone calls. While I understand there is still a certain element of that in the job, the role is far more diverse and varied. Inspectors are hugely important to the police, and are responsible for tasks such as coordinating crime solving efforts, monitoring the progress of staff and leading improvement/progress drives. Inspectors are leaders within the police force, and as such need to operate in a manner which commands respect, but also*

*presents them as someone who is trustworthy and approachable. As an inspector, I understand that my time would be spent both out at crime scenes, and at police HQ. The role is extremely varied, and for this reason it is highly appealing to me."*

## Top tips

- Understand the police core competencies and be able to recite them word for word.

## SAMPLE QUESTION NUMBER 4

*If you were given an order that you thought was incorrect, would you carry it out?*

### Sample response

*"Yes I would. As an inspector, I understand that I will be a leader within the force, but of course I will still answer to my superiors. With this in mind, I would always respect my seniors and their decisions. However, if I thought something could be done in a better way, then I do think that it is important to put it across, but in a structured and non-confrontational manner. During a debrief would probably be an appropriate time to offer up my views and opinions if asked but I would never refuse to carry out an order or even question it during an operational incident or otherwise."*

## SAMPLE QUESTION NUMBER 5

*What do you understand by the term equality and fairness?*

### Sample response

*"It is an unfortunate fact that certain groups in society are still more likely to suffer from unfair treatment and discrimination. It is important for the Police Service and its staff to strive to eliminate all forms of unfair treatment and discrimination on the grounds that are specified in their policies or codes of practice.*

*Equality and fairness is the working culture in which fair treatment of all is the norm."*

**Top tips**

- Try to read the Police Service's policy on equality and fairness. You may be able to find this by visiting their website or asking them for a copy of it to help you in your preparation;

- Consider reading the Race Relations Act, and understand the duties that are placed upon public sector organisations such as the police.

**COMPREHENSIVE LIST OF INTERVIEW QUESTIONS TO PREPARE FOR**

Q. Why do you want to become a police inspector?

Q. What are your strengths?

Q. What are your weaknesses?

Q. What can you tell us about this particular Police Service?

Q. What do you understand by the term 'teamwork'?

Q. What makes an effective team?

Q. Why would you make a good police inspector?

Q. What do you think the role of a police inspector entails?

Q. If you saw a colleague being bullied or harassed, what would you do?

Q. What do you think the qualities of an effective police inspector are?

Q. If one of your colleagues told you that they were gay, how would you react?

Q. What have you done so far to find out about the role of a police inspector?

Q. Why do you want to join this particular Police Service?

Q. Give examples of when you have had to work as a team.

Q. What would you do if a member of your team was not pulling their weight or doing their job effectively?

Q. Have you ever had to diffuse a confrontational situation? What did you do and what did you say?

Q. What are the main issues affecting the police at this current time?

Q. What do you understand about the term 'equality and fairness'?

Q. What do you understand by the term 'equal opportunities'?

Q. If you ever heard a racist or sexist remark, what would you do?

Q. Would you say that you are a motivated person?

Q. How do you keep yourself motivated?

Q. Have you ever had to work as part of a team to achieve a common goal?

Q. If you were in the canteen at work and two senior officers began to make homophobic comments, what would you do?

Q. Have you ever made a poor decision? If so, what was it?

Q. If you were ever given an order that you thought was incorrect, what would you do?

Q. Have you ever had to work with somebody that you dislike?

Q. What is wrong with your current job? Why do you want to leave it to become a police inspector?

Q. Have you ever carried out a project from beginning to end?

Q. How do you think you would cope with the anti-social working hours?

Q. Have you ever had to work shifts?

Q. How do you think you would cope with working the police shift system?

## FURTHER TIPS AND ADVICE FOR PREPARING FOR THE FINAL INTERVIEW

- The police may ask you more generic questions relating to your past experiences or skills. These may be in relation to solving problems, working as an effective team member, dealing with difficult or aggressive people and diffusing confrontational situations. Make sure you have examples for each of these;

- Try to speak to current serving police employees of the service that you are applying to join. Ask them what it is like to work for that particular constabulary and what the current policing issues are. From their feedback take the positive points but don't use any detrimental or negative feedback during the interview;

- Try to think of a time when you have made a mistake and how you learnt from the experience;

- Don't be afraid to ask the interviewer to repeat a question if you do not hear it the first time. Take your time when answering and be measured in your responses;

- If you don't know the answer to a question, then be honest and just say 'I don't know'. This is far better than trying to answer a question that you have no knowledge about. Conversely, if your answer to a question is challenged, there is nothing wrong with sticking to your point, but make sure you acknowledge the interviewer's thoughts or views. Be polite and never get into a debate;

- You will be scored against the current police core competencies, so make sure you try to structure your answers accordingly. The police core competencies are the first thing you should learn during your preparation.

\*\*\*\*\*\*\*\*\*\*\*\*\*\*\*\*\*\*\*\*\*\*\*\*\*\*\*\*\*\*\*\*\*\*\*\*\*\*\*\*\*\*

**Need further help preparing?**

**Attend a one-to-one training session with a former MET police recruitment trainer in Kings Hill, Kent.**

**Skype sessions also available.**

**To find out more, or to secure your training, contact the How2Become team today at: info@How2Become.com**

\*\*\*\*\*\*\*\*\*\*\*\*\*\*\*\*\*\*\*\*\*\*\*\*\*\*\*\*\*\*\*\*\*\*\*\*\*\*\*\*\*\*

Get Access To

# FREE

## Psychometric

## Tests

**www.PsychometricTestsOnline.co.uk**